CAIRO

CAIRO

My City, Our Revolution

AHDAF SOUEIF

B L O O M S B U R Y

LONDON · BERLIN · NEW YORK · SYDNEY

First published in Great Britain 2012

Bloomsbury Publishing Plc
50 Bedford Square
London
WC1B 3DP

www.bloomsbury.com

Bloomsbury Publishing, London, Berlin, New York and Sydney

A CIP catalogue record for this book is available from the British Library

ISBN 978 0 7475 4962 8 (hardback edition)
ISBN 978 1 4088 2607 2 (trade paperback edition)

10 9 8 7 6 5 4 3 2 1

Typeset by Hewer Text UK Ltd, Edinburgh
Printed in Great Britain by Clays Ltd, St Ives plc

For Laila, Ahmad Seif, Mona, Sanaa,
Manal, Alaa and Khaled

CONTENTS

A Note on Spelling Arabic Sounds in Latin Characters ix

Acknowledgements xi

PREFACE xiii

EIGHTEEN DAYS
25 January–11 February 2011 1
Map of Cairo 2

AN INTERRUPTION
Eight Months Later: October 2011 61

THE EIGHTEEN DAYS RESUMED
1 February–12 February 2011 119
Map of Central Cairo 120

EPILOGUE 183

Notes 195

A Note on Spelling Arabic
Sounds in Latin Characters

Writing some of the sounds of Arabic in Latin characters has been an issue since the Middle Ages. Systems of transliteration vary, along with their levels of complexity.

What I've chosen here is to adopt a new system which was, I believe, initiated by Arab bloggers. It's very simple:

1. Where there is a traditional accepted – and unique – spelling in Latin letters for an Arabic sound I retain it. As in: gh for غ – like the French 'r'; kh for خ – as in the Scottish 'loch'.

2. Three sounds are written as numerals:
The hamza, ء, pronounced as a glottal stop in the middle or at the end of a word, is written as a 2. So, if we were doing this in English, the cockney 'butter' would be written 'bu2er'. The ain, ع, a soft vibration in the back of the throat, is written 3. The 'heavy h' ح, is written 7.

However, where words already had an image and a presence for the reader of English I've kept them as they are. So 'Tahrir' has not become 'Ta7reer', 'Ahmad' has not become 'A7mad', 'Aida' has not become '3aida', and so on.

Acknowledgements

My first thank you has to go to my UK publishers, Bloomsbury, who have waited fifteen years for my Cairo book. I hope they won't be let down by what they've got.

I thank Alexandra Pringle, my editor and friend, who phoned me in Tahrir in February to tell me the moment for this book had come. Without her tenacious support and subtle judgement I don't think I'd have completed it.

I've had a novel in the pipeline for years – too many years. I thank LuAnn Walther, my editor at Knopf, for her patience and the understanding that made it possible for me to wholeheartedly turn my attention to *Cairo*.

Since 2000, the *Guardian* newspaper has been the British home for all my reportage and commentary on Egypt and the Arab world. That space has been of central importance to me at every level. I thank all the editors I've worked with there.

My Egyptian publisher, Ibrahim al-Moallem, and his editorial team at *Shorouk* newspaper, bullied me into producing a weekly column. It's thanks to them that I've found my Arabic writing voice (hand?), a whole new audience, and the opportunity to serve the revolution.

I thank: always my agent, Andrew Wylie, and my friends at his London office; Anna Simpson at Bloomsbury for racing the book through a ridiculously short publication schedule with unfailing professionalism and patience; my friend, the amazing author and poet, Adam Foulds, for saving the day by carrying proofs from Doha to London; my dearest friend and guardian angel, Susan Glynn, for reading drafts – always with my best interests at heart; Ismail Richard Hamilton, my son, and my family and friends who had to put up with having overlong out-of-context bits anxiously read out to them at inappropriate times.

Finally, Omar Robert Hamilton, my son. His critical acumen, forceful opinions, artistic sensibility and thoroughness have been invaluable as I've struggled to produce my first sustained piece of work since the loss of my husband, Ian Hamilton; my mother, Fatma Moussa; and my friend and mentor, Edward Said. I am incredibly grateful to have him.

Preface

Many years ago I signed a contract to write a book about Cairo; my Cairo. But the years passed, and I could not write it. When I tried it read like an elegy; and I would not write an elegy for my city.

Then, in February 2011, I was in Tahrir, taking part in the revolution, and reporting on it. Alexandra Pringle, my friend and publisher, called me; this, she said, must be the moment for your Cairo book. I fought it. But I feared she was right.

I say 'feared' because I wanted more to act the revolution than to write it. And because I was afraid of the responsibility. Jean Genet, in his book that I most admire, *Un captif amoureux*, writes: 'I am not an archivist or a historian or anything like it . . . This is *my* Palestinian revolution told in my own chosen order.' I cannot say the same. This story is told in my own chosen order, but it is very much the story of *our* revolution.

It proved impossible to sit in a corner and write about the revolution. What was happening, what *is* happening, needed and needs every one of us to be available at all times to do whatever the – let's call it 'the revolutionary effort' might need; whether it's marching or standing or talking or mediating or writing or comforting or articulating or . . . So I tried to 'revolute' and write at the same time and I soon realised two things: one, that I could not write what was fast becoming the past without writing the present. Two, that for this book to be as I wanted it to be and believed it should be, an intervention, rather than just a record, it needed to take in – and on – as much of this present as possible.

A revolution is a process, not an event. And, as you know, our Egyptian revolution is ongoing. And its path has not been smooth. How could it have been when the interests we are seeking to break free of are so powerful and so pervasive?

But we were given, we were vouchsafed, eighteen golden days; eighteen days when we all pulled together to get rid of the head of the regime that was destroying us and our country and everything we held dear; eighteen days that brought out the best in us and showed us not just what we could do but how we could be. And it was this way of 'being', as well as what it achieved, that captured the imagination of the world; that made the Egyptian revolution an inspiration for the people's movements that are crystallising across the planet. Every Egyptian I know is both proud of this and humbled by it. I know I am.

So it's with pride and humility and confidence and fear, but above all with solidarity and hope, that I put this book before you.

Ahdaf Soueif
Cairo, October 2011

EIGHTEEN DAYS

25 January–11 February 2011

EMBABA

ZAMALEK

OUR HOUSE

5th May bridge

SIMONDS

AGOUZA HOSPITAL

BOULAC

The hospital where I was born

MASPERO

ATABA

6th october bridge

TAHRIR SQ

gasr el nil bridge

ABDEEN

LAZOGHLI

gasr el aini st.

CAIRO UNIVERSITY

university bridge

← PYRAMIDS

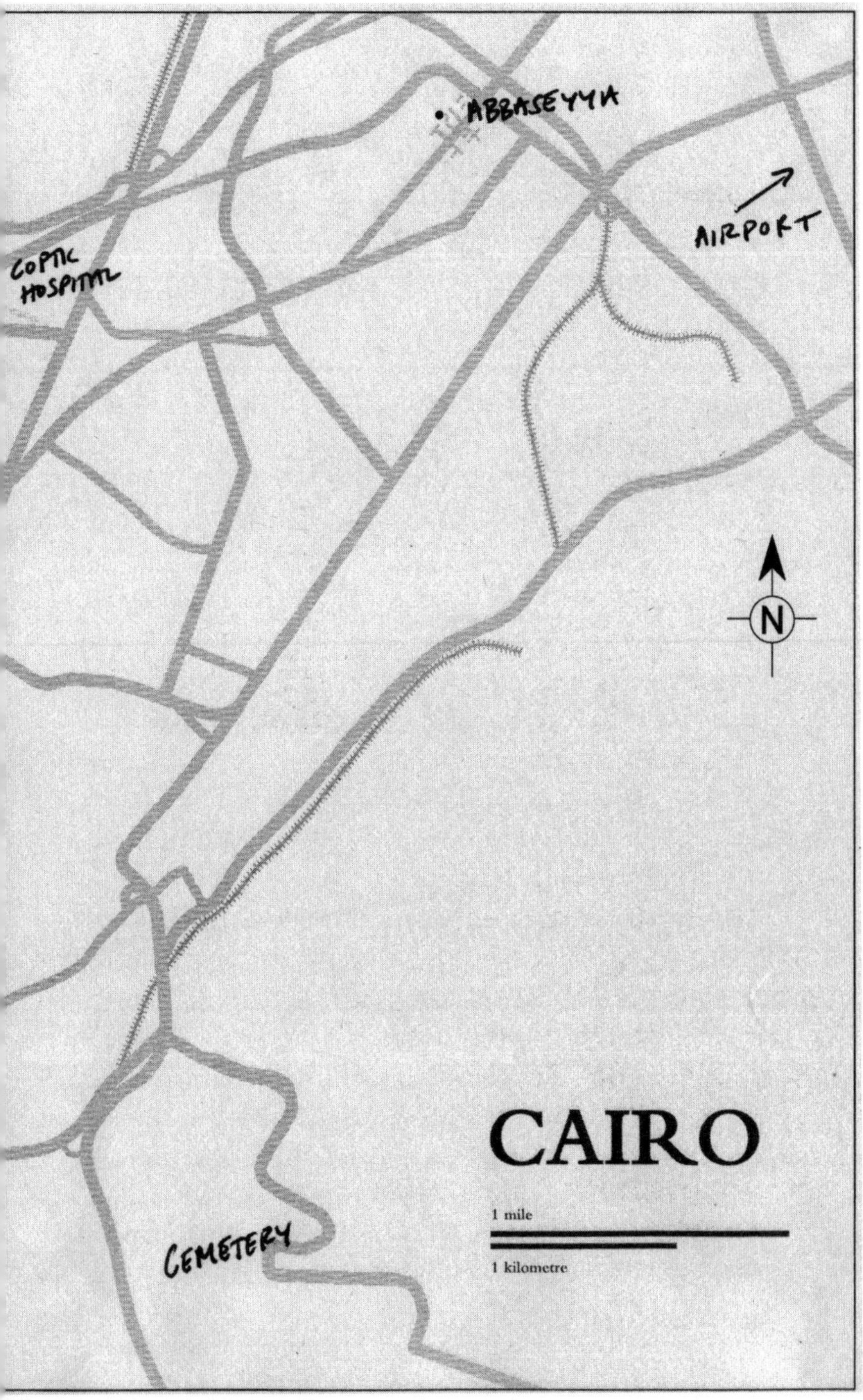
ABBASEYYA
AIRPORT
COPTIC HOSPITAL
CEMETERY
N
CAIRO
1 mile
1 kilometre

Friday 28 January, 5.00 p.m.

The river is a still, steely grey, a dull pewter. Small scattered fires burn and fizz in the water. We've pushed out from the shore below the Ramses Hilton and are heading into mid-stream. My two nieces, Salma and Mariam, are on either side of me in the small motor boat. As we get further from the shore our coughing and choking subsides. We can draw breath, even though the breath burns. And we can open our eyes –

To see an opaque dusk, heavy with tear gas. Up ahead, Qasr el-Nil Bridge is a mass of people, all in motion, but all in place. We look back at where we were just minutes ago, on 6 October Bridge, and see a Central Security Forces personnel carrier on fire, backing off, four young men chasing it, leaping at it, beating at its windscreen. The vehicle is reversing wildly, careering backwards east towards Downtown. Behind us, a ball of fire lands in the river; a bright new pool of flame in the water. The sky too is grey – so different from the airy twilight you normally get on the river at this time of day. The Opera House looms dark on our right and we can barely make out the slender height of the Cairo Tower. We don't know it yet, but the lights of Cairo will not come on tonight.

A great shout goes up from Qasr el-Nil. I look at Salma and Mariam. 'Yes, let's,' they say. I tell the boatman we've changed our minds: we don't want to cross the river to Giza and go home, we want to be dropped off under Qasr el-Nil Bridge.

And that is why we – myself and two beautiful young women – appeared suddenly in the Qasr el-Nil underpass among the Central Security vehicles racing to get out of town and all the men leaning over the parapet above us with stones in their hands stopped in mid-throw and yelled 'Run! Run!' and held off with the stones so they wouldn't hit us as we skittered through the screeching vehicles to a spot where we could scramble up the bank and join the people at the mouth of the bridge.

That day the government – the regime that had ruled us for thirty years – had cut off our communications. No mobile service, no Internet for all of Egypt.[1] In a way, looking back, I think this concentrated our minds, our will, our energy: each person was in one place, totally and fully committed to that place, unable to be aware of any other, knowing they had to do everything they could for it and trusting that other people in other places were doing the same.

So we ran through the underpass, scrambled up the bank and found ourselves within, inside, and part of the masses. When we'd seen the crowd from a distance it had seemed like one bulk, solid. Close up like this it was people, individual persons with spaces between

them – spaces into which you could fit. We stood on
the traffic island in the middle of the road. Behind us
was Qasr el-Nil Bridge, in front of us was Tahrir, and
we were doing what we Egyptians do best, and what
the regime ruling us had tried so hard to destroy: we
had come together, as individuals, millions of us, in a
great cooperative effort. And this time our project was to
save and to reclaim our country. We stood on the island
in the middle of the road and that was the moment I
became part of the revolution.

A month before, a week before, three days before, we
could not have told you it was going to happen. Yes, there
had been calls to use National Police Day on 25 January
as an occasion for protests, but there had been so many
protests and calls for protests over the years that it hadn't
seemed special. Those of us who were in Egypt intended
to join, for form's sake and to keep up the spirit of opposition. Those of us who weren't – well, weren't.

Me, I was in India, at the Jaipur Literary Festival. Late
on the 24th I did an interview with Tehelka TV:

> . . . for a very long time now, our perception is that
> [Egypt] is not being run in the interests of the Egyptian
> people. And the primary motivation of the people who
> are governing us is that they should remain in power in
> order to continue ransacking and looting the country.
> Now, the main support that they have to remain in
> power is of course the Western powers – particularly
> the United States. And the price that they pay in order
> to be supported is to run policies that favour Israel.

We've been watching what's been happening in
Tunisia and we've been very excited by it. You hear:
now, will Egypt move? And you hear: Egypt is too
big . . . too heavy.

It really does not look as if the government is going
to allow a peaceful and democratic change. So . . .
what's going to happen? Will we get a situation where
people . . . sort of, erupt? And you get . . . blood on the
streets? And will the army come down? Nobody knows.
It feels very unstable. And it feels dangerous. And all the
activism that happens is in specific areas. And it's all
young people and it's all really without a leadership . . .
but it's there. It's keeping the streets alive. We've never
had as much civil unrest in Egypt as we've had in the
last five years. And that is good. That is good – but,
how will it coalesce? And what shape will that take?[2]

We now have this information. You, my reader, in
more advanced form as you read these words than I as I
race to write them in the summer of 2011. I won't try to
guess at what's on your news bulletin today – but whatever shape Egypt is in as you're reading now, this is the
story of some of the moments that got us there.

And it's also, in a small way, a story about me and my
city; the city I so love and have so sorrowed for these
twenty years and more. I am not unique; but Cairo is.
And her streets, her Nile, her buildings and her monuments whisper to every Cairene who's taking part in
the events that are shaping our lives and our children's
futures as I write. They whisper to us and tug at our
sleeves and say: this is where you were born, this is

where a man, a boy, first reached for your hand, this is where you learned to drive, this is where the picture in your schoolbook shows Orabi facing down the Khedive Tewfik, this is where your mother says she and your father stood in '51 and watched the fire take hold of Cairo. The city puts her lips to our ears, she tucks her arm into ours and draws close so we can feel her heartbeat and smell her scent, and we fall in with her, and measure our step to hers, and we fill our eyes with her beautiful, wounded face and whisper that her memories are our memories, her fate is our fate.

For twenty years I have shied away from writing about Cairo. It hurt too much. But the city was there, close to me, looking over my shoulder, holding up the prism through which I understood the world, inserting herself into everything I wrote. It hurt. And now, miraculously, it doesn't. Because my city is mine again.

'Masr' is Egypt, and 'Masr' is also what Egyptians call Cairo. On Tuesday 1 February, I watched a man surveying the scene in Tahrir with a big smile: the sun was shining and people were everywhere, old and young, rich and poor, they talked and walked and sang and played and joked and chanted. Then he said it out loud: 'Ya Masr, it's been a long time. We have missed you.'

It was evening on Tuesday the 25th when I realised something was happening back home. On my Jaipur hotel TV I could only get CNN, but there the Americans were, transmitting from Tahrir, and the whole world was wondering what was going on, and the spokesperson for the Egyptian government, Hosam Zaki, was cheerily dismissing the crowds we were watching on the screen and reassuring the world that our government and our people were very close and the government knew the people and knew what they wanted and would supply the bits of it that it saw fit. This was the line that the regime was unable to let go of; throughout the three weeks of the confrontation every speech given by (now deposed President) Mubarak or his Vice-President, Omar Suleiman, or any member of his party or regime maintained the patronising 'we know what's best for you' stance that had been so roundly rejected by the people.

What transfixed me so completely was that the picture on the screen was from Tahrir. Unmistakably from Tahrir. Midan el-Tahrir —

I prefer the Arabic word, 'midan', because, like 'piazza', it does not tie you down to a shape but describes an open urban space in a central position in a city, and the space we call Midan el-Tahrir, the central point of Greater Cairo, is not a square or a circle but more like a massive curved rectangle covering about 45,000 square metres and connecting Downtown and older Cairo to the east, with the river and Giza and the newer districts to the west; its southern boundary is the Mugamma3 building and its northern is the 6 October Flyover —

The Midan has been our Holy Grail for forty years. Since 1972 when (then President Anwar) Sadat's forces dragged the student protestors at dawn from around the empty plinth at its centre and into jail, demonstrations and marches have tried and failed to get into Tahrir. Two years ago we managed to hold a corner of a traffic island in front of the Mugamma3 building for an hour. We were fewer than fifty people, and the government surrounded us with maybe 2,000 Central Security soldiers, the chests and shoulders of their officers heavy with brass.

Since Egypt's ruler Khedive Ismail established it in 1860 – its core modelled on Paris's Étoile, six main roads leading out of its centre and a further six out of the larger space surrounding it – control of Tahrir has seemed central to controlling the country. Ismail himself stationed the Egyptian army and the Ministry of Defence here, and when the British occupied Egypt in 1882 their army took over the barracks and the Ministry on one side of Qasr el-Nil Bridge and they put their embassy on the other. The Americans were to follow suit and put their increasingly fortress-like embassy next to the British. Then in Nasser's revolutionary times Egypt put a statue of Simón Bolívar between the two embassies; the Arab League building and the headquarters of the Arab Socialist Union went up in place of the British barracks, and the Ministry of Foreign Affairs faced them from the (nationalised) palace of the Princess Nimet Kamal across Tahrir Street.

But as well as housing the symbols of military and political power, Tahrir is home to the civic spirit of Egypt. The Egyptian Antiquities Museum (1902) marks the northern end of the Midan, and when in 1908 the Egyptian national movement founded – through public donations – the first secular Egyptian University, they rented the palace of Khawaga Gianaclis – now the old campus of the American University in Cairo – at the other end. In 1951 the government decided to consolidate all its departments that the citizen directly dealt with in one central building, and so Mugamma3 al-Tahrir was built. And, early in the

1952 revolution, the small mosque near the Mugamma3 was enlarged and dedicated to Sheikh Omar Makram, the popular leader against Napoleon's French Expedition in 1798, the British 'Fraser' Expedition of 1807 and, later, against Muhammad Ali himself when he felt the ruler was taxing the people unfairly. Omar Makram died in exile but his statue was part of our revolution; a meeting place, an inspiration, a bearer of flags and microphones and balloons.

In 1962, the first modern international hotel in Egypt, the Nile Hilton, opened in Tahrir, next to the Arab League. Eight years later, on the evening of 27 September 1970, and having just closed the two days of negotiations and arm-twisting that ended Black September and killed him, President Gamal Abd el-Nasser – whose picture was raised by many during the revolution – stood on the balcony of the thirteenth-floor suite he had occupied for a few nights and gazed at the Nile. He turned, smiling, to Abd el-Meguid Farid, the Secretary to the Presidency: 'How come I've never seen this amazing sight before? Look at it. I'm buried alive out in Heliopolis.' Then he went home. And it was from a window in the Arab Socialist Union next door that, two days later, his wife and daughters watched his funeral surge across Qasr el-Nil Bridge towards Tahrir. This is the building that became Hosni Mubarak's National Democratic Party headquarters – the only building in Tahrir to be torched by the revolutionaries.

The Hilton – now bearing the Ritz-Carlton sign – has been undergoing renovation for years. In front of it is a waste ground surrounded by sheets of corrugated iron

– which we will use in the battles for the Midan. This massive space in the central midan of our city has been in this ruined condition for twenty years. We are told it's to do with the construction of the Metro. Also to do with the Metro, we're told, was the removal of the empty plinth in the middle of the garden of the central round-about, the plinth around which the students gathered in 1972 on the night Amal Dunqul wrote of in 'The Stone Cake':

> *Five o'clock struck*
> *with soldiers a circle of shields and helmets*
> *drawing closer slowly . . . slowly . . .*
> *from every direction*
> *and the singers in the stone cake clenching*
> *and relaxing*
> *like a heartbeat!*
> *Lighting their throats*
> *for warmth against the cold and the biting dark.*
> *Lifting the anthem in the face of the approaching guard.*
> *Linking their young, hopeless hands*
> *a shield against lead*
> *lead*
> *lead.*
> *They sang.*

Now, the whole country is gathered around that central, plinthless garden. In one of the most moving moments of the revolution – and there were to be many – the people's delegations that had come in from the cities and the provinces to the Midan set up their banners and set up the

chant: 'El-shar3eyya m'nel–Tahrir' – legitimacy comes
from Tahrir.

I got myself to Delhi in the morning and, next day,
caught a plane that put me in Cairo in the evening on
Thursday the 27th. From the airport I called my sister,
Laila, and asked: 'Where's the revolution? Should I go
to Tahrir?' She said I should call her daughter, Mona,
and Mona said there was nothing in Tahrir but I might,
possibly, see some crowds if I went to Midan el-Sa3ah
in Nasr City or if I drove through Abbaseyya. But
there were no crowds. I saw two charred and over-
turned Central Security Forces trucks but the city was,
if anything, quieter than was normal for a Thursday
evening. The revolution was up and running in Suez
and Alexandria; in Cairo it was gathering its breath,
getting ready for Friday.

Friday 28 January, midday

Embaba, on the western bank of the Nile, five minutes
and one bridge from my home on Gezira Island. For a
long time all I knew of it was the name of its main bus
stop, the 'Kit-Kat', and attached to the name a black-
and-white image of British 'johnnies' staggering out of
shady doorways, drunk, into the street, hushed families
watching them from darkened rooms, their faces lined
with the light from street lamps falling through drawn
blinds. The Kit-Kat, I seemed to know, was one of the

many sleazy nightclubs that had sprung up in Cairo to cater to the Allied forces stationed there in the West's second great war. Now, if you say 'el-Kit-Kat', everyone thinks of Daoud Abd el-Sayyed's 1991 film with the opening shot of Mahmoud Abd el-Aziz weaving through the Embaba streets on his bicycle. A long, continuous shot – and some time during the course of it you realise the cyclist is blind.

Embaba has a small airport from where you can go gliding. When my first marriage was breaking up we flew from there, in a glider, I and my just-become-ex husband. He was at the controls. I can't think why we did that. For clarity, maybe? We – I – didn't find it. Even the amazing spread-out fields below, the river, broad and still and – from here – docile were dimmed by my unease.

And Embaba is known for three hospitals. One is a specialist rehabilitation centre where they taught the five-year-old son of Um Nagla, our help, to speak. My father snatched him back from the jaws of a 'fraudulent charlatan', he said, who was about to send him off for electric shock treatment – and sent him to Embaba. He's now fifteen and speaking plenty. He says he'd carry on going to school if there was any use, but he's not learning anything and the teachers are only there for the cash from the private lessons. The only thing that might be useful now for his life is the revolution. He berates his mother for being prepared to believe that Hosni Mubarak is 'sorry' and will give back our stolen money. 'Ali,' she tells me, 'Ali says of Mubarak and all his men: "Before they open their mouths they're liars; they breathe lies." And this,' she adds, 'is Ali-who-couldn't-speak.'

The second is the Embaba Fevers Hospital which used to rival the best in the world. The third is the new Emergency Hospital where building was stopped when its riverfront position caught Mrs Mubarak's eye and the government decided to turn it into a luxury residential block. The latest scandal of this kind is the Madinati Project where 8,000 acres were sold at so much lower than market price that the courts estimated the loss to the Egyptian Treasury at billions of pounds. Today as our protest passes the hospital project the crowd starts up the chants against corruption: 'A bowl of lentils for ten pounds – a Madin'ti share for fifty p.'

We've been walking the streets of Embaba for two hours. My friend, Mamdouh Hamza, brought me here and left me in a small coffee shop by the local mosque. MH is a celebrated civil engineer who's been in charge of some of Egypt's major construction projects. I'd known he'd been lending his support for a while to some of the revolutionary shabab, the young people. 'Something will begin here,' he said, and went off to distribute banners. It was the usual pleasant, the world-is-on-pause feel of Friday prayer time and I watched the women chatting in front of shops, the winter sunshine falling on them through the colourful clothes displayed above their heads, the men sitting at cafés, others spilling out of the mosque, praying on green mats in the road. In my coffee shop a young man is sitting in the corner; something about his stillness, his quality of concentration, stays with me.

Prayers finish but the imam solicits blessings. And blessings. And more blessings. Men start folding their mats, putting on their shoes. Suddenly the young man from the coffee shop is above the crowd, on top of it. People shift and stir, there's a buzz like in the theatre at the moment the curtain starts to rise, everyone looks, people come out of shops: the young man's arm is in the air, his hand is reaching to the sky, and there comes the loud, carrying voice: 'Al-sha3b yureed isqat al-nizam!' There it was, no lead-up, no half-measures; the young man on the shoulders of his friends; a loose knot of some fifteen young people: 'The people – demand – the fall of this regime!' We start to walk.

Later, we will learn that similar marches started after prayers in every district of Cairo and many other cities. We will know this young man as one of the three hundred young people who organised these first marches. Up there, his still concentration has transformed into energy, his back is straight, his arm movements are precise. Again and again the call goes out, and the crowd responds: 'Your security, your police – killed our brothers in Suez.' We walk and the numbers grow. Every balcony is full of people; some just watch impassively, some men look uncomfortable. 'Come down from the heights / Come down and get your rights', most women are smiling, waving, dandling babies to the tune of the chants: 'Eish! Horreyya! Adala egtema3eyya!' Bread. Freedom. Social justice. Old women call: 'God be with you! God give you victory.' For more than two hours the protest walks through the narrow residential lanes, cheering, encouraging, instigating: 'Prices up and no one cares / Next you'll sell your beds and chairs.' We pass the offices of the Land Registry. In 2008 I'd visited it to get some papers relating to my mother's estate. I failed to get them.

At the next window a man remonstrated that this was the fifth time he'd been and that he no longer understood what he was required to do to get the stamp he needed on to his papers. Then he lost it: 'Yel3an abu Hosni Mubarak!' he bellowed, 'God curse him curse him curse him!' He slammed his files rhythmically on the counter top as he cursed out the man at the head of the system that, here and now, in this local specific manifestation of petty bureaucracy and corruption, was frustrating him to insanity.

'Eish! Horreyya! Karama insaneyya!' Bread. Freedom. Human dignity. Kids run alongside the march: 'The *people – demand* – the fall of this *regime*—' In the eighties and nineties, at the time of the big expansion of the Islamist currents, Embaba came in for some particularly harsh treatment. The Dakhleyya (Ministry of the Interior) stopped policing Embaba itself but set up border stations at its exits; every male going in or out was subjected to stop and search. Anyone not carrying his ID was detained, and detained meant beaten – sometimes tortured. Several times during today's march, sweeping up people from the neighbourhood, the cry rises: 'To the police station!' and each time the march's leaders deflect it.

Later I will find out that my sister, Laila, MH, and various other friends were all on this march. But it had grown so big we didn't see each other. By the time we wind on to a flyover to head for Downtown we are easily 5,000 people or more.

As we descend from the flyover I recognise that we're in Ahmad Orabi Street. This is where my beloved Khalu, my mother's brother, ever present though gone now these

eighteen years, used to live. His wife still lives here. I
glance up at her plant-filled balcony and I can't resist. I
slip away from the march and up the five floors to her flat
where I find cousins and friends – all have slipped away
from the march for a few minutes' rest and to find out the
news. We'd woken up that morning to find the Internet
down, and by 11.00 a.m. not a single mobile was working.
Landlines were all we had, and, even there, the international lines had been taken down. We knew then that this
was a regime fighting for its life. We sat around in Tante
Nahed's home and used her landline to phone around and
check up on friends and family. Most homes had arranged
to have one person stay in by the landline and act as liaison.
My brother when I called him said his daughters wanted
to join the action, and would I take them? This would be
their first protest. Tante Nahed gave us tea and juice. The
last time I'd sat in her living room was two years ago and
I had been looking through the results of a survey she'd
just published: *The Problems and Discontents of the Egyptian
Citizen*. Unemployment consistently scored highest on the
list of people's personal problems, second was housing and
third was education.

4.00 p.m.

My brother, Ala, and his wife, Sohair, and their daughters, Salma and Mariam, pick me up. As we drive we
pass protests heading to Tahrir. Ala and Sohair have

brought bottles of water and hand them out. Months later,
my brother – an IT man and Egyptologist – will, with
friends, put together an initiative to dismantle the security
establishment, another to overhaul pre-university education, another to set up a national employment bureau . . .
Today, this is his and his wife's first action for the revolution.

Salma and Mariam and I decide we'll walk across
6 October Bridge and up the Corniche into Tahrir, so
my brother drops us off in Agouza, at the foot of the
steps leading up to the bridge. We run up the steps and
find ourselves facing a cordon of Central Security soldiers
blocking our way. The bridge crosses Gezira Island and
passes over the Gezira Club. My nieces, twins, had both
been champion gymnasts in their childhood and teens and
the Gezira was their club. Now twenty-two, they could
easily still pass for seventeen. I take their elbows and stride
up to the line of soldiers: 'Excuse us, my daughters are late
for their training—' pointing below us at the club grounds.
The line opens courteously.

I love these young men. I love them, and I don't want
them to be part of Central Security. In fact we've got a
case in court proposing that using conscripts for Security is
unconstitutional; conscription may be necessary to protect
us against invasion or aggression. But to use conscripts
to protect the government of the day against the people
cannot be right.

We get to the middle of the bridge before we realise
that there are no cars, that the air is dim and fumy and
that the few people around us are not moving forward.
There's something of Dante about the spectacle. Isolated

figures drift. Smoke drifts. Everything is slowed down and dim. A young man comes up and gives us tissues, then sprinkles vinegar over them. 'Hold them over your nose,' he says, 'a tip from our Tunisian friends.' In Palestine they use onions. We can't yet smell the gas. I see a friend, Lena, and her husband, and we drift together, embrace and stand silently watching a man wearing a large brown paper bag over his head rotate slowly on the narrow traffic island at the centre of the bridge. He's turning in slow motion and as he faces us we see the slits for the eyes and the large, red question mark starting on the forehead and running down the nose with the dot at the mouth. Later I realise this is the first piece of revolutionary street theatre we see. Now, it just adds to the weird, dreamlike feel of the scene. A heavy thudding thumps rhythmically through the smog. Lena says it's guns. Across the water we can see that the real action is on Qasr el-Nil Bridge. We've started to feel the gas but Salma and Mariam and I decide to follow our plan and run the hundred metres or so to the bridge's exit by the Ramses Hilton, get down and run along the river to Qasr el-Nil.

Tear gas! This was a gas that made you feel the skin peeling off your face. Later, when we saw the canisters, we found it had passed its expiry date. You'd think that would make it less painful but apparently it makes it worse. We run and I can't even open my eyes to see what's going on. When I do force them open for a second I see that Mariam, the more delicate of the twins, has stopped in the middle of the bridge, her eyes streaming and shut tight, one of her shoes lost, her arms held out helplessly. She's saying something but so softly I can't hear. Salma and I run back for her. 'I can't,' she's whispering, 'I can't.' We find her shoe, grab an arm each and run. We run down the slope of the bridge and straight into another cordon of Central Security soldiers. They're meant to block the way. We are three women, dishevelled, eyes streaming. We run right up to them and they make way. 'Go!' they urge us. 'Quick!' Eye to eye with one of them, young, brown, open-faced, Egyptian, I pause, just for a second. 'What can we do?' he shouts into the smoke. 'If we could take off this uniform we'd join you!'

Stuck. Stranded. For a moment as I was running down the slip road with my eyes closed holding on to my nieces I had the – typical – thought that we might nip into the Ramses Hilton and wash our faces, maybe even get some tea. Down on the embankment, with the soldiers facing us and behind them the Corniche road littered with stones and charred cars and the Hilton dark and shuttered, it was clear that a five-star interlude was out of the question. We run down the embankment steps and jump into a boat: to Giza, please. Drop us next to Gala2 Bridge. We'll go home.

But: as we get further from the shore our coughing and choking subsides. We can draw breath, even though the breath burns. And we can open our eyes. And when our eyes meet we change direction and head, again, to Tahrir.

On the traffic island at the Qasr el-Nil entrance to Tahrir you turned 360 degrees and everywhere there were people. I could not tell how many thousands I could see. Close up, people were handing out tissues soaked in vinegar for your nose, Pepsi to bathe your eyes, water to drink. I stumbled and a hand under my elbow steadied me. The way ahead of us was invisible behind the smoke. From time to time there would be a burst of flame. The great hotels: the Semiramis Intercontinental, Shepheard's, the Ramses Hilton, had all darkened their lower floors and locked their doors. On the upper-floor balconies stick figures were watching us. At the other end of the Midan, from the roof of the American University, the snipers were watching us, too. Silently. Everywhere there was a continuous thud of guns and from time to time a loud, intermittent rattling sound. We stood. That was our job, the people at the back: we stood and we chanted our declaration of peace: 'Selmeyya! Selmeyya!' while our comrades at the front, unarmed, fought with the security forces. From time to time a great cry would go up and we would surge forward: our friends had won us another couple of metres and we followed them and held our ground. We sang the national anthem. Eight months ago some young protestors from the 6 April Group had been arrested in Alexandria for singing the national anthem; it was 'instigatory' the prosecution said. We sang it. On 28 January, standing at that momentous crossroads, the Nile behind us, the Arab League building to our left, the old Ministry of Foreign Affairs to our right, seeing nothing up ahead except the gas and smoke and fire that stood between us and our capital, we stood our ground and sang and chanted and placed our lives, with all trust and confidence, in each other's hands.

Some of us died.

Many of us had not yet truly realised what we were
engaged in; what the country was engaged in. We knew
that Suez had been under siege for three days and people
there had been killed. We knew Alexandria was up, and
news was coming in of other cities. But we were still calling what we were doing 'protesting' – and we had been
protesting for ten years. I think that every time I've arrived
in Cairo – and that's three or four times a year – I've
joined my sister and various friends on protests: marches
to support the Palestinian Intifada, marches against the war
on Iraq, protests against our rigged elections, our co-opted
judiciary, against the plots to perpetuate the regime by
slithering Gamal Mubarak into power, against corruption
and against police brutality. The government was vicious
in dealing with all of them. It knew that a demonstration for Palestine or Iraq would sooner or later turn its
attention to the Egyptian regime, and that a demonstration
against the regime would count its role in Palestine and
Iraq among its sins.

Looking back now we see the progression, from small
groups collecting medicines for the Intifada, to the civil
movement, 'Kifaya', hitting the streets, to the massive
workers' strikes in Mahalla, to the point where every
sector in civil society – judges, lawyers, farmers, teachers, pensioners, journalists, tax collectors – was fighting
with the government. And I see it, too, in my family.
Like so many 'politically engaged' Egyptian families it's
now in its third generation of activists – and this third
generation, in their twenties, are more clever and cool
and effective than we ever were. We, the older revolutionaries, have been trying since '72 to take Tahrir.

They are doing it. They're going to change the world. We follow them and pledge what's left of our lives to their effort.

Friday 28 January, 10.00 p.m.

Four army tanks are on the Maspero[3] Corniche, the run of riverside from Boulac to the Ramses Hilton on the eastern bank of the Nile, five minutes and one (different) bridge from my home on Gezira Island. They're blocking the road in front of the Radio and Television building (known, through metonymy, as 'Maspero') where, when I was a student, I had my first job. I played 'Laila' who, with her brother 'Ahmad', appeared in weekly episodes of a sitcom designed to teach English to schoolchildren. Sometimes we filmed on location, but mostly we worked in a studio in Maspero. This was in the early seventies, and the cavernous and freezing 'Studio 6' had no editing facilities. Each episode was twenty minutes and we had to record it from start to finish without stopping. If someone made a mistake or missed a cue or got the giggles we had to start from the beginning. And if our booked time ran out we had to vacate the studio and wait till a free slot came up and try again. So I've spent many, many hours loitering in this area, re-warming myself, drinking tea and chatting and hanging about and catching up on essays and assignments. And now it is dark and deserted and there are four army tanks outside the building and MH is distributing molasses sticks to both the soldiers on the tanks and the revolutionaries on the street 'for energy'.

In the weeks to come I will understand why revolutions and coups always rush to seize the radio and television facilities. Our revolution seized the main midans of our cities and went on to deal with the strongholds of the most hated parts of the regime: its party and its brutal security establishment. Next day there was talk of Maspero, but trying to take it would have meant engaging not the police or Central Security but the military.

At 6.00 p.m. Hosni Mubarak had declared a curfew. Nobody paid attention. At 7.00 p.m., while the battle for Tahrir was raging, a cry – a jubilant warning – had gone up: 'El-geish nezel!' The army had deployed. We saw the first open four-man vehicle arrive on the Corniche by Qasr el-Nil Bridge and just about caught a glimpse of the red berets of the Military Police before the welcoming, co-opting crowds closed in on the vehicle.

Now, at ten, we walk past Maspero and past the darkened Ramses Hilton. In the eighties it was a novelty to zoom up thirty-six floors and watch, from 'Windows on the World', as night fell and strings of city lights blinked on and light-encrusted boats darted about on that central darkness that was the river. Five days from now the regime will barricade the world's media correspondents in this hotel while it calls in its cavalry and makes a desperate stand against the revolution. But we don't know that yet. Ahead of us a huge cloud of black smoke rises to the sky: the National Democratic Party headquarters has been set on fire; flames leap from its windows and the windows of Suzanne Mubarak's Specialist National Councils. Hundreds of people on Qasr el-Nil Bridge are holding up mobile phone cameras. But, next door, around the Egyptian Museum, the young people, the shabab,[4] have linked arms and are surrounding the building, cordoning it with their bodies. When the fire broke out next door even young people who had left the Midan came back to protect the Museum. At this point none of us knows that the regime's snipers are concealed on its roof. We don't know that the army will use it as a holding pen and a fast-torture location. The young revolutionaries just know that it's their Museum and they have to protect it; they will not move until they have handed it officially to the army. They even make the brigadier with his tanks show ID before they'll give him the building.

When I'd gone home to drop off Salma and Mariam and to write and file copy, my aunt Laila Moussa (Lulie) said that Mona and some of her friends had stopped at the house and taken some clothes and papers and that they're locking themselves away in someone's mother's unused apartment. They've managed to establish a connection to the Internet. The young man who's hacked through to the Net is blind. Mona is twenty-four. Throughout the revolution she will race between Tahrir, her genetics lab at Cairo University where she's finishing her M.Sc., and the secret location where she and her band of friends become the central nerve in the great communication effort that keeps the revolution linked to itself and to its comrades in the world outside. Now Lulie says Mona had phoned on the landline to say that there was a small mosque in the Tahrir area that was receiving the wounded and anyone who could help in any way should go there. Lulie herself is a doctor, but we persuaded her to wait, wait till morning before trying to go out.

MH insists that we skirt Tahrir so we go down Mahmoud Bassiouni and Tal3at Harb to get to the back of the Midan, and here, as we walk through Downtown, the sense of being in a film hits me. One of those urban apocalypse movies where the familiar features of Manhattan – it's generally Manhattan – are eerily recognisable through the flood/hurricane/nuclear destruction. The streets, the buildings are the same but they're dark and semi-empty. The shops are shuttered. Litter seems to be floating around at knee level. There's rubble on the streets and the lights are out and there's no police: no traffic police, no guards on banks, nothing.

In neighbourhoods across the country, through the night of this Friday that will become known as the Day of Wrath, the regime killed hundreds of Egypt's young. Police and Security men drove cars and trucks into groups of protestors.[5] Snipers shot young men and women from the rooftops of the Ramses Hilton, the American University, the Egyptian Museum and the Dakhleyya. Troops fired on them with shotguns and rifles and automatics, the thug militias, the baltagis, burned them with Molotov cocktails and battered them with stones, ceramics and marble. Soldiers broke down and cried and were comforted by the revolutionaries.[6] Families will spend months of heartbreak finding out and trying to prove how their children were killed. Brave doctors and lawyers will speak up for them. The Dakhleyya will continue – as I write – to deny responsibility.

Now, in the darkened and derelict heart of our city, we come out in Midan Bab el-Louq. And because we're out of communications we don't know that, three streets down, the young people, the shabab, are taking on the well-hated Dakhleyya; attacking the massive, fortified building in Lazoghli with their bare hands, improvised weapons, and the anger of many years.

When my aunt Awatef (Toufi) got married she moved into a flat in Lazoghli. I was eight years old and I used to go and stay with her often, and so, alongside 'Ataba' and 'Abdeen', my childhood landscape acquired the oddly named 'Lazoghli'. Odd because of the tickly effect of the heavy 'z' and the 'gh' so close together, and because – unlike 'Ataba' and 'Abdeen' – it wasn't a word that meant anything in Arabic. Soon, I learned that 'oghli' was Turkish for 'son of'; I would demonstrate precocity in front of my parents' Leftist friends by saying I was staying at 'Lazovitch'.[7]

Unlike Ataba which was always connected with bustle and commerce, and Abdeen which was the royal and then presidential palace, exclusively Lazoghli for me was the bridal setting up of a new home; a home that was an alternative to how my parents did things.

When my mother was twelve she fell ill with rheumatic fever. This meant that she got to lie on sofas and read while her nine-year-old sister had to step into the traditional domestic role of eldest daughter. These roles were to last all their lives: Fatma ('Fifi', and, later, 'Mama Fifi') the brainy intellectual, Toufi the keeper of tradition.

So when she married and moved to Lazoghli, Toufi's flat was a demonstration of the proper way of doing things. Though small, it had a 'salon' (drawing room) and 'sofrah' (dining room) – the two pillars, it seemed, of every Egyptian household (except my parents') and whose very names reflected the two dominant cultures to which the Egyptian bourgeoisie was in thrall: French and Turkish.

The drawing-room chairs were upholstered in pale blue brocade and the windows had soft white cotton curtains – which, when Toufi and her husband moved back into the family home a few years into their marriage to look after my grandfather, had to be extended by double their length to fit her old windows. When she died nine years ago, and we had to dismantle the Ataba house and I washed and folded the curtains, I realised that the repeated pattern of three slim horizontal pleats halfway down each curtain had been her solution to disguising the joining seam. I sat with the curtain on my knee and the pleat between my fingers and thought how she had always done that: made do and patched up and fixed the world with results of originality and elegance.

But Lazoghli, most importantly, had a balcony where, on summer nights, we had a full view of the screen of the open-air 'Cinema Lazoghli'. No bedtime, no restrictions on what you could watch – the absence, when it comes down to it, of my father's regulations: Lazoghli was freedom with a prime seat at a summer cinema every night. From here I watched *River of Love*, *The Other Man*, *Rumour of Love*, *A Beginning and an End* . . .

My aunt, as I said, moved back to Ataba and Lazoghli dropped off my map for decades. Until, in 2000, when

Egyptians started mobilising in support of the Palestinian Intifada, it came back: 'Lazoghli' was disappearances, 'Lazoghli' was torture, 'Lazoghli' was the Dakhleyya and the State Security Intelligence Bureau, the 'Mabahith Amn el-Dawlah'. It was also the Coroner's Office which habitually covered up the crimes of the Dakhleyya and the State Security Intelligence Bureau.[8] Now – unbeknownst to us in Bab el-Louq, three streets down – the young revolutionaries are attacking Lazoghli, and the security establishment, about to lose the streets of the country, is determined to keep Lazoghli. Five snipers are on the roof, snipers whose existence the ministry will deny despite their images captured on film.[9]

As we stand in Bab el-Louq I can hear a voice over a tannoy. I can't make out the words but the voice is repeating them and repeating them and it sounds like an appeal. It comes from the Midan end of Tahrir Street where I expect Mona's mosque to be so I start walking up towards it. It's dark and the shop on the corner with the best carob juice in town is shuttered. MH has gone to hunt for a truck that will agree to come here and transport the wounded. Men walking down warn me to turn back. I can hear the shots and smell the acrid smoke, but a lesson learned from time spent in Palestine is that unless there's an insurmountable physical obstacle (and that includes a man or woman with a gun) keep going. So I keep going and find that the voice is coming from Amir Qadadar Street to my left: 'This is a house of God. A house of God and a hospital. There are wounded people here and doctors trying to help them. You must not attack this house. Your brothers and sisters are here. This is a house of . . .'

It's an entrance you might easily miss. One of the magical architectural features of downtown Cairo is the pedestrian passages that run between or through buildings. My grandfather's house had one of those. You walk through them, under cover, linking from street to street. Some of the wider passages have stalls or shops. This entrance is to a passage that links Amir Qadadar Street to Tahrir. I didn't know it existed and I only see it because of the knot of people and cars outside it. 'This is a house of God – and a hospital—' the voice declares and there's rubble and smoke and the only people in the street are around that small entrance almost hidden by a large sign for mobile phones so that's where I go. I edge past the hurried toing and froing and I'm inside and the space is maybe twenty metres long by eight metres wide. If I walk straight through I'll come out on the east side of Tahrir, but to my left there's a waist-high railing that runs the length of the passage and the space beyond it – a width of some six metres – is a small mosque. Well, not a proper 'mosque' but a space that has Qur2anic verses hanging on the freshly painted walls, and a prayer niche to guide you towards Makkah, and rows of prayer mats on the floor, and on the mats there lie young men covered in blood, and other young men are running in through the Midan entrance carrying yet more young men covered in blood and lowering them carefully on to the mats and by the walls figures are stretched out shrouded in dark blankets and then I see a white light at the centre of it all and it's coming from a slight figure crouched on the floor doing something to the chest of a young man, and the figure has a face of such intent seriousness and compassion that

I cannot look anywhere else and I stand and watch her until she finishes and straightens up and is revealed to be Mona Mina, one of the leaders of Physicians Without Rights and my sister's friend and the mother of a fiery and popular activist. I step towards her and a young man runs up between us and puts his head in my eye line. As I say 'journalist' he's asking: 'Is the pellet still there? Can you take it out or should we leave it? I have to get back to the shabab.' The shabab are storming the Dakhleyya. Mona tells me she knows two of the young fighters: 'Two weeks ago they were scared to report that their boss was bullying them. Look at them now!'

I look. Wounded young men everywhere. And other young men and women tending to them. Medicines and dressings stacked in neat piles by the walls. People come to talk to me. I write fast; their message is urgent: they're using live ammunition. They're using shotguns. Look: empty cartridges. Made in the USA, look. Look: his legs aren't working. Two have died. No one wants to go to hospital because they report them and they get taken away. Eye injuries. Head injuries. They're shooting to kill. Then the tear gas floods in again and the exhortations on the loudspeaker grow louder, disbelieving, almost angry: 'Soldiers of Egypt! Police of Egypt! Your brothers and sisters are in the protection of this house . . .' Young men try to carry the wounded out into the air through the back. Someone gives me a gas mask. Someone else gives me two empty cartridges. They'll sit on my mantelpiece. 'This is what we get from US AID. This is the "aid" they hold over us.' The gas clears. A collapsed Central Security soldier is carried in. He's given emergency treatment and his weapon is emptied before he's set free. He sobs as an older man pats his shoulder. Weeks from now we'll find out that soldiers went AWOL and lived on the Midan until the military broke the sit-in. I make a list of things the hospital needs: Betadine, dressings, spray anaesthetic, sutures, needles, surgical gloves, painkillers . . .

At midnight I'm standing outside the pharmacy on the street corner opposite my house waiting for the pharmacist to bag the things I've bought and for MH to come back from his search for sutures and needles. We suspect we won't get these because pharmacies are not allowed to sell them except to hospitals. We drove to a couple of hospitals and they wouldn't let us in. The central twenty-four-hour emergency pharmacy is closed. So we've gone round collecting things from any neighbourhood pharmacy that's open. There are no street lights. And no police.

The Dakhleyya, thoroughly beaten by the protestors in Alexandria and Suez, and about to lose Cairo, has pulled all its men from the streets. The accepted figures for the personnel of the security establishment is about 1.5 million. They have received orders to withdraw from duty. Our government has switched off the lights and gone away. Actually, no; they've not gone away: in the dark they've thrown off the camouflage and transformed into the occupying force they always were.

Word is coming through that the Dakhleyya is closing down selected jails and police stations across the country and letting – or even throwing – violent criminals out. In el-Wadi el-Gedeed prison all the cells were opened except for one which held thirty-six newly detained Islamists, then the prison was set on fire. A group of convicted criminals risked their lives to break open the cell and set the new prisoners free. We'll find out later that General Muhammad al-Batran, the Dakhleyya's Chief of Intelligence of Prisons, has been battling to keep order. General Batran has a reputation for fairness. Yesterday he visited Fayyoum prison and established peace there. It will turn out that at the same moment that I'm standing here, on the corner, waiting for the medicines, he's on the phone to his sister. He is enraged. He tells her that Habib el-Adli, the Minister of the Interior, has closed down seventeen police stations and is going to set the whole country ablaze. Tomorrow General Batran will go to Abu Za3bal prison and restore order. Then he'll go to Qatta prison and talk to the prisoners and they will agree to return to their cells – and then he will be shot and killed by the Inspector in charge of the jail. His sister, Manal al-Batran, will pursue his killers in the courts for months – perhaps years.

I glance up and my balcony, on the sixth floor, draws my eyes to its light, its trellises and plants. I always leave the light on at night, so that I, coming home, or someone coming to visit, can glance up and feel an early welcome. Now I question whether it's a good idea.

Karima comes to talk to me. She is my age and she's the daughter of the greengrocer under my building. He, the greengrocer, used to sit quietly in the corner all day with a cigarette-full of hashish while K's mother ran the shop and the children. When I was small I used to watch their fights from the balcony – enthralled. They were a

mother and a father with two daughters and a son. Just
like us. But instead of the tight lips, the silences, the 'withdrawal of affection' that signalled anger or displeasure in
our household, their emotions and exchanges were all
out there: yells and wails and tantrums, the mother chasing the kids with a bamboo cane, the kids screaming and
running and dodging behind startled passers-by, the street
intervening, cuffing them on the head, enforcing peace.
I was sure I preferred their style to ours. The parents are
dead now and the brother runs the greengrocer's. He still
gets into fights and the classy glass front he's put up for his
shop is often smashed. But K owns three hardware and
general stores on the street and holds court from a stool
on the corner. When her children were young you saw
them stop by her; composed and well dressed and always
carrying books.

She comes to talk to me and she says she's worried.
'They drove round and collected all the guards from the
embassies and the banks,' she says, 'and it's not only that;
they've turned their baltagis loose on the streets. How can
we live without security?'

'Don't tell me you're afraid?' I joke.

'Of course I'm afraid.'

'Well, seriously, don't be. You could take on a hundred
baltagis.'

The baltagis are worse than the regular forces. They're
men – and recently women – with a record of violent
crime, who're trained and paid by the Dakhleyya and used
for special assignments, like beating people up at elections,
dispersing protestors, etc. A baltagi is mercenary and without honour. A baltagi is violent and loud but ultimately a

coward; his speciality is bullying the weak. And K is not weak.

Two weeks later, when Mubarak fell, she took off her galabeyya and veil and put on a loose trouser suit and a scarf. When I grinned she shrugged: 'Just a bit of a change.' But at midnight on 28 January we stand together and watch three young residents armed with sticks take up position outside my apartment block. 'Where are your children?' she asks. 'They're coming,' I say. I don't tell her that I've made my youngest, Ismail Richard, stay put in London to circulate information and help organise the protests there – and finish his MSc. But my older son, Omar Robert, is, in fact, trying to come home. Two nights from now he will join these young men at the barricades.

As we'd driven from Tahrir to my neighbourhood, Zamalek, to look for pharmacies, news was coming through of the police withdrawal. By the time we'd finished buying the medicines and were heading back to Tahrir we passed three citizen checkpoints in Zamalek alone. In every district people came down from their homes and set up neighbourhood watches, 'Popular Committees'. They invented barricades out of tyres and chairs and lengths of wood and blocks of stone and traffic barriers. The characters of the checkpoints varied with the neighbourhoods: in the villages they were farmers with axes and hoes; in the poorer neighbourhoods they wore galabeyyas and carried sticks; in the posh districts they had walking canes and golf clubs; at one Zamalek checkpoint there was a lady in a camping chair hold-ing a glass of gin and tonic. Kids played in the streets. For a week the city was policed by Popular Commit-

tees; they had fun, checking ID and licences and ushering
cars through with a theatrical flourish. Everywhere they
were courteous and apologised for the inconvenience.
And we were courteous right back and thanked them
for protecting us, thanked them for giving us our city
back. Everybody ignored the curfew. People, especially
women, say they'd never felt more safe. We joked, seriously, that we could save the eighteen billion pounds the
Dakhleyya cost us every year and put it into something
more useful. In the daytime the shabab ran the traffic
and collected the litter. Revolutionary graffiti started
to appear everywhere, and became more confident and
more sophisticated each day.

2.00 a.m.

It is quieter at the mosque. I deliver the supplies, add them
to the neat mounds that other citizens have brought in,
then sit with an exhausted young doctor who tells me he'd
come down with four of his friends from Minya to join
the protest. They had lost each other and, with no mobiles,
couldn't communicate. Then the shooting started and he
knew what he had to do. He had been working non-stop
for ten hours. I ask if he knows where he'll sleep. My
brother, who's come down with more medicines and a
car, takes him to the Hisham Mubarak Legal Centre which
is now functioning as a shelter and food kitchen as well as
providing legal back-up for activists. The Centre was set

up by my sister's husband, Ahmad Seif, and a group of friends in 1999, and named after one of the group, Hisham Mubarak, who was thirty-five when he had died of a heart attack ten years earlier.[10] Tonight its floors, its sofas are home to scores of Egyptians from outside Cairo who've come to join the revolution.

Before I leave I ask the name of the mosque. It is the Mosque of the Servants of the Compassionate.

Hundreds died that Friday night. And thousands were injured, and many died later of their wounds. Their smiling, hopeful faces are everywhere. Our shuhada: Our Martyrs of the Revolution, who walked in peace and died before they could live the lives they dreamed of. Their song becomes our anthem.[11] We march in their funerals and we promise 'We'll get what they died for / Or die as they died'. If we tire or our hope dims, our optimism for a moment falters, we open our hearts and they come to us: their bright faces, their hopes, their lives, their parents, their children. This is now our life's work: we will create the Egypt they died for.

3.00 a.m.

On my way home I walk again through Cairo's darkened streets, through the rubbish, past the shuttered shops and the closed hotels and the smouldering Party headquarters and the charred, upturned personnel carriers, and it all seems apt. It's not a film any more. This is the reality that we've been living for decades, finally risen to the surface. At last our capital reflects the true condition of the country and of our lives: burned and broken and almost ruined. And now we'll have to save it.

I come again to the four tanks on Maspero. The soldiers in camouflage are still standing on top of them; I wonder if they have to stand there all night or if they may at least sit down. Behind one of them is the sign of the Paprika restaurant and as I look at the restaurant's dark-ened window I see – so clearly that my breath catches – I see my younger self, ablaze with love and poetry and the stormy, dusty khamsin winds, sitting, leaning, across the table from the man I love, the man who has followed me from London to Cairo, allowing him to hold my palm to his mouth, to kiss it under the gaze of all the waiters standing by.

For our honeymoon we drove up the length of the Suez Canal and only discovered we were on a military road when we hit the first checkpoint and it was too late to turn back. The soldiers fetched the Colonel. I gave him our passports, our story, our marriage certificate from the day before. He stared for a moment at the silent foreigner in sunglasses sitting in the passenger seat, then he said 'Mabrouk' and let us pass. We went through at least ten checkpoints before the road gave us an option to exit.

Four months later our London wedding, for good or ill, is on the anniversary of Nasser's 1952 revolution. And my life becomes Cairo/London, London/Cairo. And both cities change, but I like – on the whole – the changes that happen to London: the view from Waterloo Bridge; more exciting every year, the blossoming street markets, the angel alighting once more on the dome of our local theatre. In Cairo, every time I come home, home goes a bit more bitty on me.

I come home and find the old mysterious villa on the corner of our street gone. One of my classmates used to vanish into it at the end of every schoolday; now the wrought-iron railings, the dense trees, the lights shining far within: all gone. In its place this pharmacy.

I come home and they've pulled apart my beloved Abu el-Ela Bridge and built the ghastly 15 May Flyover in its place. No more strolls to Maspero, to Boulac, to the Shagara Café. The flyover (named after the 1971 coup – the 'Corrective Revolution' with which Sadat consolidated his power and got rid of what was left of Nasser's men) runs across Zamalek, and turns its high street into an instant slum.

In Ataba, the other main theatre of my life, the changes were more radical. A super-ugly iron walkway circumambulated the midan: Midan el-Ataba el-Khadra, the Place of the Green Threshold. Step through the threshold, east into the heart of the old city, west into the heart of Haussmann's late nineteenth-century creation, both hearts centred on commerce. Everyone here was in small industries and trade. But they used to have style. My grandfather's home was here, his business a five-minute walk across Shari3 el-Azhar. But he was dead, and Khalu, my uncle – because of the Mafia-style practices of the tax authorities – was shifting the business from wood to aluminium. The showrooms and workshops, soon to be sold, were in the massive Italianate terrace on the eastern side of the Midan. Look at the confidence of it! Of the National Theatre, and the Khedivial Post Building, and the block which held Matatias's coffee shop where Khalu played chess every night.

And the house: a solid Mediterranean-style apartment block fronting on a quiet courtyard on Shari3 el-Geish. The fun thing was to approach it from the other side, from the Ruwei3i market. You walked through the busy street past Alf Sanf w'Sanf, the piled-high toy store from which we bought all my toys and my brother's and sister's toys. Alf Sanf w'Sanf furnished me one day with the sudden aperçu that the accurate translation of 'Alf leila w'leila' was not the literal 'A Thousand and One Nights' but just 'A Thousand Nights' – or even 'Lots of Nights'. Anyway, past the toy store and through the cool passageway that runs under the building and you emerged in a courtyard with notices and banners hanging out to dry outside a calligraphy workshop, then you turned right into the spacious entrance with the old black-and-white marble floor and the stately wooden lift. This was the landscape that furnished my imagination and kept me going through the cold years of the Ph.D. in the north of England. When I came back I fought my way through the Ruwei3i market to find my aunt, Toufi, fighting a battle with rising garbage and falling plaster and smashed marble. The lift had been overpainted with brown lacquer and street vendors run by the local MP were using the entrance as storage. Of our neighbours, older people were dying, their children moving into the new districts, away from the centre, their apartments taken over by local bosses who used them as storage for cheap goods, and baltagis.

Cairo/London, London/Cairo, and Cairo was being constantly downgraded. Despite the new luxury multi-purpose blocks, the marble shopping malls, the $15 million apartments, the city was disintegrating. Part through neglect and part, I felt, on purpose. Streets were dug up and left unpaved. Sidewalks vanished. Prime and historic locations – like the site of the burned-down Opera House just off Ataba – became car parks. Street lights dimmed. Nothing was maintained or mended. Old houses were torn down and monstrous towers built in their place. Public transport became a joke. And in a noose around the city they built luxury gated communities on virtually stolen land, adorned them with water-guzzling golf courses and called them 'European Countryside' and 'Beverly Hills'.

And through it all I loved her and loved her more. Millions of us did. We'd wake up one morning and find a just finished underpass dug up again, more marble and ceramics brought in to line its walls. We'd check out which MPs traded in marble and ceramics (the same MPs who will send truckloads of baltagis with marble and ceramic shards to crack open our heads in the streets of the revolution). Traffic signals were burned out and bent and we'd wake up another morning to find the city had sprouted plastic palm trees festooned with wink-ing red and green light bulbs. They'd really scored there: not only made money but made Cairo into a clown. We apologised to her. Amongst ourselves and in our hearts. We told her we loved her anyway, told her we're stay-ing. I felt a rush of love every time I passed the strange, creamy house with the rotting turrets which they hadn't yet pulled down; the great art deco cinemas, flea-ridden and on their knees but still there. The day the Cairo tower lost its discreet white uplighting and was caught in a net of flashing coloured dots I cried. They dammed sections of the Nile to create new waterfront residences (the Ministers of Housing responsible are now being tried) and land was sold from under residents' feet to foreign 'investors'. Cement was poured into every public construction project, including disastrous restorations of thousand-year-old mosques. The cement factories ran on subsidised fuel and made a profit margin of 65 per cent. In Muqattam the sewage from a new, wealthy development on the top of the hill eroded the rock on which Dwei2a, the old poor district below, was precariously perched and sent it crashing down the jagged hillside (the residents are now camped in protest in front of Maspero, their wretchedness displayed for all to see). A quarter of a million children lived on the streets and some people set up shelters for them and some made films about them and some stole their kidneys and corneas. Police officers ran protection and drugs rackets. People regularly fell out of windows during questioning or had heart attacks in police custody. There was a video of a woman hanging upside down and begging, begging . . . there were protests, marches, demonstrations every day. There were flash screenings of torture videos. The top judges of the country stood for two hours in silence in the street outside the Judges' Club with their sashes and ribbons and medals on their chests. We knew then that judgement would surely come.

Degraded and bruised and robbed and exploited and mocked and slapped about: my city. I was ashamed of myself for not saving her. Every one of us was. All I could do was look and listen and stay and march and insist that I loved her. And she acted like she didn't care. She unravelled with bravado. Every thread of that once tightly ordered pattern breaking loose: blue and green and red and black and every shade and texture, all sprung away from the tapestry, in disarray, tangled, knotted, vivid, sizzling, present. The city stayed awake longer, put more people on the streets. It threw up new haphazard districts and when the government would not supply them with water or electricity people stole them from the mains. It opened special restaurants and started special services to cater for the new Gulf tourists. Including agencies for seasonal marriages to young, pretty, impoverished Egyptian women.

Small art galleries opened, and tiny performance spaces; new bands formed across the musical spectrum. Mosques and cultural centres clutched at the derelict spaces under flyovers. Green spaces vanished but every night the bridges would be crammed with Cairenes taking the air. We suffered a massive shortage of affordable housing but every night you'd see a bride starring in her wedding procession in the street. Unemployment ran at 20 per cent and every evening there was singing and drumming from the cheap, bright, noisy little pleasure boats crisscrossing the river.

Trees that were not cut down refused to die. They got dustier, some of their branches grew bare, but grew. We looked out anxiously for the giant baobab in Sheikh Marsafy

Street in Zamalek, for the Indian figs on the Garden City
Corniche, for what my kids called the Jurassic Park trees
by the zoo. If they cut a tree down it grew shoots. If they
hammered an iron fence into its roots the tree would lean
into the iron, lean on it. If a building crowded the side of
a tree the tree grew its other side bigger, lopsided. I knew
trees that couldn't manage leaves any more but put all they
had into a once-a-year burst of pink flowers. And once
I saw a tree that seemed looked after, that had just been
washed: it couldn't stop dancing.

I loved her. I would wake up in my London bed
convinced that as my front door opened on to Wimbledon, my garden door opened on to Zamalek. Until one
day, when I was neither in Cairo nor London but in
Jaipur, the shabab of Egypt decided they would no longer
allow their lives to be stolen, and in every district in the
country they got up and walked into the hearts of their
cities. They chanted: 'We're your sons / And daughters
too / What we're doing is for you' and we came down
from our houses and walked with them. They marched for
bread and they marched for freedom, for social justice and
for human dignity. We followed them and we marvelled
at them and we stood shoulder to shoulder with them and
every so often – more often than they wanted, for sure –
we'd grab one of them and hug them and shake their hand
and thank them. Yes, we would thank them for lifting the
burden of failure from our backs; for ridding our hearts of
their load of sorrow, for stepping forward and sweeping
away the question that tormented each one of us: what
manner of homeland, what manner of future am I leaving my children? What have we allowed to happen to our

country? To our world? We're taking care of it, they said, just stay with us: 'Parents! Friends! Draw close to us!' And we did.

Sunday 30 January

MH has turned his office into a revolutionary headquarters and this is a meeting of some of the older figures of what you might call the establishment opposition to the regime of Hosni Mubarak. Most are over sixty-five. They sit in a big circle and the buffet man goes round with coffee. They talk above each other and only listen long enough to pick up a line and go with it themselves. An unkind thought crosses my mind: this is the political leadership that failed. They talk about the necessity of creating a patriotic front to fill the vacuum created by the fall of the National Demo-cratic Party, about the need to call for the election of a founding committee to write the Constitution – and the conversation/argument has the same theoretical feel as the ones we've been listening to for thirty years: lists of things we need to do. But our host has promised us a visit from some of the young leadership of the revolution; when they come in an energy comes in with them. Six young men, all in their twenties. They're like a football team; they huddle and confer quickly, they 'pass' to each other with a nod or a look. They're concise, self-deprecating, firm and courte-ous. They say that if they claim any credit it would be for 20 per cent of the people who came out on the 25th; the

rest has been spontaneous, organic – as surprising to them
as it was to everybody. When the Khaled Said[12] Facebook
page received over 300,000 responses to the call to come
out on the 25th, eleven other groups decided to meet and
coordinate. They met physically (and secretly) and organised themselves and their friends. They are about three
hundred and, no, they don't all know each other. They
won't give information about how they operate but they
want to put it on the record that, were it not for all the
protests and writings and activism of the older leadership,
they would not have been able to do what they're doing
now: 'We've learned from you,' they tell the room, 'and
we're building on what you've accomplished.' There's
a silence, and then one of the older people says simply:
whatever you want us to do, we'll do.

I go out on to the porch. If I walk across Mesa7a
Street to the right I'll come to a house we lived in briefly
when I was three. A memory of riding a blue tricycle
down a paved slope into a – living room? My mother
at a sideboard wearing a full-skirted dress in blue and
white pencil stripes. The walls are ablaze with paintings,
and in the living room my parents' friends, the authors
of these paintings, all in their twenties, are laughing
and arguing and waiting for the mini sandwiches my
mother is preparing at the sideboard. This is the university neighbourhood. Just down the road there's the Cairo
University Faculty Club – the Union. We used to come
with my parents when we were children and play in the
garden while they socialised or organised. My parents
taught at Cairo University all their lives and Laila, my
sister, followed them – only she specialised in maths. In

2006 she was one of the group that founded the 9 March Group for the Independence of the Universities – and she and her comrades started contesting the Union. As she told of stormy meetings, of regime-rigged elections, of being locked out of the building and holding alternative meetings on the pavement outside, I would try to imagine all this happening in the quiet, lofty rooms with their dark furniture, their rugs, their discreet lighting that spoke so sonorously of stability and scholarship and calm. And now, just as my eight-year-old self is peeping around a heavy wooden door into a book-lined room, I hear an earth-shaking roar and low down in the clear, blue winter sky four F-16s are circling and swooping. They circle several times. In Tahrir it turns out people had started to dance: 'He's gone crazy! He's gone crazy!' they sang, and danced the crazy dance.[13] A man who works for MH comes on to the porch: 'Don't go to Tahrir,' he warns, 'go home and stay there. This whole story they're talking about inside isn't going to work.' I remind him there's a call for a millioneyya[14] tomorrow. He says he has a friend in the innermost circle of the Presidential Guard. 'They have a plan for this. They've been getting ready for it for a long time and now,' he says, 'they have orders to put the plan into action: they're going to do dirty things, terrible, terrible things. It's going to be over in two days. Please believe me.' The wide white steps lead down into a beautifully kept garden where a calligrapher is busy at work on a series of huge banners: 'IRHAL!', 'IRHAL!', 'IRHAL!'. Go!

In the sky above Tahrir an hour later helicopters circle and tilt, circle and tilt, and on the ground we tilt right back at them, all of us, waving and laughing and holding up our banners for the men in the machines to read.

Mubarak has extended the curfew – and the Midan is teeming with hundreds of thousands of people and more and more are coming in. He announced a Cabinet reshuffle with General Ahmad Shafiq as Prime Minister – and Tahrir chanted: 'The People Demand the Fall of this Regime.' Yesterday, when he appointed Omar Suleiman as his Vice-President the Midan roared: 'No Mubarak / No Suleiman / No more umala amrikan' (agents for America), and on the front of the papers this morning Mubarak and Suleiman going through the swearing-in ceremony look irrelevant, even unreal. This is what's real; what's happening here: the citizens flooding into Tahrir, the cheers, the chanting, the waving banners, the sense that we are pushing against something that will give. We don't know when, but it will give.

So we carry on, we chant and we sing and we wave the flag and then again we're all looking up at the sky because the air around us is growing dim and heavy and the sky darkens and darkens and then the thunder comes. God's thunder. It rolls and booms above our heads. Again and again it comes and then lightning cracks the skies open and the deluge pours down on us. We stand in awe. Thirty minutes of rain fast and fat and furious and then the sky, the air, the city clears. The sun comes out and Tahrir sparkles and leaps to life. 'Allahu Akbar' rolls across Cairo. God is with us; He has sent us a sign and has cleansed our skies of Mubarak's jets.

And Omar Robert, my older son, flies in. After a nail-biting interlude when they said the plane would not land in Cairo but would fly back to Athens they change their minds and he arrives. It takes us two hours to get from the airport to Zamalek. The army has closed off the section of highway that runs past Mubarak's residence – even though he's in Sharm el Sheikh – so we have to drive through side streets and, everywhere, the Popular Committees have set up their barricades. Omar has his first taste of the revolution. We show IDs, licences, everybody thanks everybody. At midnight he goes down to volunteer for the barricade on our street. In a little while he comes back. 'I have to have a weapon,' he says, 'and I don't fancy a kitchen knife.' He roams the house looking troubled. Then, leaning against the hall stand, he finds what he's looking for. My son patrols our street armed with my mother's walking stick.

And I am left to remember the times I walked into this flat to find my sons chatting with my mother on the balcony, or in the kitchen being fed, and how we moved from my mother pushing their swings or watching over them by the pool to Omar driving her around the streets of Cairo and – a couple of times – to the little orchard by the Pyramids that she loved so much.

Tuesday 1 February

I shall park by the small building that I still think of as the Pocket Theatre. In the mid-sixties my mother used to drag me here to see experimental productions of

Beckett and Brecht and Aeschylus. I loved the Nile-side neo-pharaonic building in its grove of palm trees and I liked being part of an evening activity, a 'grown-up' activity. But after the already-too-long performances there would be intense discussions as to whether Brecht should be in colloquial Egyptian or modern standard Arabic, whether Shakespeare's sonnets had to rhyme in Arabic, whether Sophocles or Euripides were more useful for our times, whether you could – in a transla-tion – add a phrase that changed no meaning but fixed the rhythm. I was SO bored. But something stayed with me – something to do with, shall we say, believing that artistic endeavour matters – that it's worth arguing about, and that it can (should?) have an intimate rela-tionship with the world it happens in. Something to do with responsibility.

There's no parking to be had. The space is crammed, in every nook and cranny there are BMWs, beat-up old Fiat 128s, sleek Mercedes, environmentally unfriendly 4 x 4s, responsible Toyotas; everybody's parked and come to join the revolution. I find a spot down the alley by the Ahli Football Club, cross and walk past the Andalus Gardens and over Qasr el-Nil Bridge. Families of four generations are walking into Tahrir on a brilliant, sunny Cairo day.

The entrance to the Midan is a tangle of tanks, barbed wire, soldiers and people. Yesterday, the twelve entrances to Tahrir were guarded and the sit-in secured by shabab from the Popular Committees. Today it seems the army's helping. At the Qasr el-Nil entrance we hold up our IDs as one by one we squeeze through the narrow gaps between the tanks. It doesn't feel good. Soldiers stand above us as we squash ourselves through their hardware. But they look friendly, and on Sunday, after the air force buzzed us, the Supreme Council of the Armed Forces, SCAF, declared that the armed forces would never fire on the Egyptian people.[15] Battalions of people are continuing the charm offensive that started on Friday – they surround the tanks, lean on them, climb on to them, paint them, stick flags and flowers on them, throw their babies to the men manning them; every tank is overwhelmed, every officer and soldier engaged in conversation, in photo-ops. Last night there was a football match – the people versus the army – with a tank as the prize. The people won. They didn't get the tank. But an officer emerged on to the Midan; young, rugged, well-spoken and almost in tears, he made a speech urging us not to leave our positions until we'd got everything we wanted. He was lifted on to people's shoulders and carried round the Midan: 'The People! / The Army! / One Hand! / The People! / The Army . . .'[16]

I tell non-Egyptian friends, journalists, interviewers who ask that we're not Greece or Latin America; that the Egyptian army is very much part of the fabric of Egyptian society, and in both 1977 and 1985 it refused direct orders to fire on Egyptian demonstrators. An oath taken by every soldier is that he will never raise his weapon in an Egyptian face. The army says it will secure for us this space where we are carrying out our peaceful, democratic, young, inclusive, open-source, grassroots revolution. My parents' generation warn us; they send messages through their children, our friends: take care. Don't trust the army. My sister quotes the proverb 'Harras wala tkhawwensh' – Don't assume treachery, but be on guard! And in any case, what are our options?

Mubarak is holding on. The Dakhleyya is working against us; they have already killed at least 145 people and news is filtering through of killings in jails, of bodies found on highways, of attempted robberies of state institutions, of arson – all conducted by men officially and unofficially on the payroll of the Dakhleyya. Next-door Libya's erupting, Sudan to our south is breaking apart and to our east there is Israel, always Israel; Israel which is declaring its concern for Mubarak and calling him a strategic asset – which we've always known and is a large part of our problem with him. And in between us and all this stands our army: our brothers and husbands and sons. They're not 400,000 and they're spreading themselves thin. Since the 25th they've had to deploy rapidly through Egypt's twenty-six governorates, and now they have to be in the cities as well. And we believe that they're like the rest of the country: the very top levels were part of the regime and have made millions. The conscripts and soldiers are ordinary Egyptians making a meagre living. The officers and middle ranks have the same wishes, fears, angers, ambitions, equivocations as the rest of us, and on the whole would rather not see Egypt on its knees and would rather not be America and Israel's scabby mongrel allowed to shelter and feed as long as it knows its place, and would quite like to have a decent country where we take responsibility for ourselves and work to make sure everybody can have bread, freedom and social justice.

We know that the army collects a ton of US AID. We know it represents about a third of the GDP of our country – that it is a massive business interest. We know that in the army, as in the government and the state and also outside our country, there are massive – fine, the biggest possible – interests that do not wish us to do what we wish to do, that do not want for us the lives we want for ourselves. But right now we have to take the chance that the balances within the army will keep it from harming us. Right now we need to deal with the other forces ranged against us, inside and outside Egypt. The forces that want our land and our location, our resources and our position and our history and our quiescence and that want us out of a number of equations in our region and the world. They fasten on to us and feed, they spoon out our brains, our health and our will. And if we don't fight them off we shall not even die the death that is a merciful release but the death that is death-in-life: we shall be condemned to a zombie existence where we are emptied of ourselves but continue to perform their 'Egypt'.

Bread. Freedom. Social justice. How many have come to today's millioneyya? The military say two million in Tahrir. Four million across Egypt. And all these millions look like people who've woken from a spell. We look happy. We look dazed. We turn to each other to question, to reassure. A man asks: how did they divide us? How did they make us frightened of each other like that? Another man – with his hand on his son's shoulder – says to me, picking up the thread of a conversation we might have had: 'Yes, really. I thought so badly of him; sitting all day at his computer. Now look what he and his friends have done. Respect. Respect.' People have put up tents in the central garden. In one tent young women are collecting footage of Dakhleyya torture. In another, people are stacking bottles of water and dry biscuits. I lower myself to the ground for a moment's rest and see I've sat next to the covered wife of a man in the shortened white thob and the white skullcap of the Salafis. I wonder if they'll mind. He sees my glance: 'Are you looking at me because I have this beard and I'm smoking?' A wide smile: 'I just couldn't afford razors. When he leaves I'll buy all the razors I need.' We all become instant friends. And I see old friends, too; as I wander the Midan I bump into people I know are living in Brussels, in Doha, in DC, in London. Everyone has dropped everything and come home. We're walking around wide-eyed, pale with emotion. We hug. 'You too? But of course you'd come,' we say, and hug again. For a moment Omar is next to me. 'Would you have imagined the revolution would look like this?' he says. All the ills which plagued our society in the last decades have vanished overnight. Young men, who a month ago could have been thought a menace to any woman on the street, were chivalry itself. People offer each other biscuits, dates, water. People chat, people pick up litter. We revel in the inclusiveness, the generosity, the humour that come so easily to us. Students, businessmen, waiters, academics, farmers, civil servants, unemployed – we are all here together, all doing what we've not been able to do for decades: each and every one is speaking, acting, expressing themselves and insisting on being counted.

A group of some thirty fair-skinned young people are gathered by the central garden. They hand out leaflets written in Arabic, English and French. They carry a

banner that says: 'The Khawagas [Western foreigners] who
have made Egypt their home salute the revolution!'

The world's media is here. 'I don't know if one should
say this,' one journalist says, 'but it's like – it's like Wood-
stock.' She looks worried but if there'd been room I'd
have picked her up and waltzed. On an early morning
interview I'd reassured a worried BBC anchor that Tahrir
was like carnival. Another journalist is in tears: 'For thirty
years we've been discussing revolution – and if a revolution can be "good". And – here it is; you've just done it.'
I see Jon Snow and Medea Benjamin. A man pops out
of a tree with branches tied to his arms and performs a
tree dance. Another improvises a stand-up routine as 'the
Indian Expert, Mr Nana', coming to tell us how to run
the revolution. Stages have been rigged up and bands are
playing.

But there are also black ribbons flying and pictures,
pictures, pictures of the young people who were killed by
the regime in the last six days. Our shuhada.[17] Together,
we pray for them the Prayers for the Absent. 'And do not
consider those who were killed in the path of Right as
dead; for they live in the presence of their Lord, and they
prosper.'[18]

And the Midan feeds us, nourishes us: this is the Egyptian Museum that holds our ancestors, the Museum that
our shabab defended – the Museum that bears witness to
who we are. This is the Arab League – an example of the
death-in-life that was to be our fate; we will breathe life
into it. This is the plinthless space. What good fortune that
no statue occupies this central space, that the absence of a
leader is physically manifest in Tahrir, and our leaderless

revolution is watched over, instead, from the boundaries, by Omar Makram, Simón Bolívar and Abd el-Men3em Riyad. And the roads that open out from it – Champollion to the great Law Courts and the Unions, Qasr el-Eini to Parliament and the Cabinet Office and then to the great teaching hospitals, Tahrir Street to Abdeen and the Palace then to the Citadel, Tal3at Harb to town and Atabah and commerce and then the Azhar, Gala2 to the central railway station and then the Cathedral – and right next to you, running alongside you – the Nile.

In the novel I was working on before the revolution happened, there's a scene that was written in August 2007. 'Mada' is talking to 'Asya' about the Museum: 'You know,' says Mada, 'it's unbelievable. It's as if the city doesn't even belong to us. A soldier stopped me walking near the Museum in Tahrir the other day. In the centre of Cairo. He said it's forbidden to walk here. I couldn't believe it. "How d'you mean forbidden?" "It's forbidden." I pointed at a whole load of people walking into the Museum. He said they're foreigners. I said so I'm forbidden because I'm not a foreigner? Are you serious? What if I want to go to the Museum? He said why should you go to the Museum? I said haven't you noticed it's called the "Egyptian" Museum? And haven't you noticed this square is called "Liberation" Square? Do you know who it was liberated from? It was liberated from the foreigners, for us: the Egyptian people.' 'And what did he say?' 'He said: "You'll have to speak to the officer."'

A great cry goes up from the square: 'Irhal! Irhal!' (Leave! Leave!) Everybody is looking in the same direction: from the sixth-floor balcony of an art deco building a long banner unfurls, falling gracefully down the front of the building. We read: 'Leave! We want to breathe!' Holding it from the balcony is a young woman with streaming curly hair. She is jumping up and down and holding up her hand in a victory salute. The crowd salute back: 'Irhal! Irhal!'

Tahrir is about dignity and image as much as it is about the economy and corruption. It hurts how much this regime has messed with our heads, divided us, maligned us to the world. 'They say we only care about a loaf of bread,' a young labourer says. 'We care about bread. But we also care about our dignity.' Together, in the Midan, over the last four days, we have rediscovered how much we like ourselves and each other and, corny as it may sound, how 'good' we are. I sneeze and someone passes me a tissue. And all the time the chants continue, the demands are articulated, options for the future are discussed. It is not possible to say what will happen next. But I look around and I know this won't stop. No one, nobody, not one of us, is going to step back into the nightmare.

AN INTERRUPTION

Eight Months Later: October 2011

'It is not possible to say what will happen next. But I look around and I know this won't stop. No one, nobody, not one of us, is going to step back into the nightmare.' This is what I wrote eight months ago. And now, of course, we know what happened next: Hosni Mubarak fell on 11 February; we celebrated, and the world – you – celebrated with us. The Supreme Council of the Armed Forces, SCAF, with tanks on our streets, stepped forward, saluted our shuhada, declared its belief in our revolution and promised to protect it and the people and the transition into democracy. We left the Midan.

But I need to pause while we're still there, in the Midan; to interrupt this account of the eighteen days, to tell you the ongoing story of our revolution. Because the story does go on; we have not stopped, even though we may have fallen off your – off the world's – television screens, for the moment.

This book is not a record of an event that's over; it's an attempt to welcome you into, to make you part of, an event that we're still living. And there are two problems in the writing of it. One is that while the eighteen days are locked into the past, the revolution and the fight to hold on to it continue, and every day the landscape shifts. The other is that you – my reader – are in a future unknown to me, and yet I want to tell a story that will ease the leap you need to make between where this book stops and where Egypt is as you read.

As I write, I think of you holding this book and reading my words, weeks, months, into the future, and I wonder what the reality that you are seeing will be. That reality is what we, today, as I write, are working, fighting, dying in order to shape.

These are the last few hours that this, my text and I, have together; the last few hours I have to write for you, to you. And it's hard to write because things keep happening, pushing my pen this way and that, or making me lay it down as I stare out of the window and contemplate.

We've just had word that Alaa Abd el-Fattah, my nephew, Laila's son and Mona's brother, has been summoned to the Military Prosecutor to face a charge of 'Incitement and Destruction'. Alaa is twenty-nine, an IT man, an activist and blogger. He and his wife, Manal, like many of our shabab, like Omar, had been living and working abroad and dropped everything and came home to work for the Egypt of the revolution. When Mubarak was deposed Alaa and Manal decided the world was ready for their first baby. The first child of the next generation in our family will be born, God willing, on 24 November. Alaa is at a conference in San Francisco. And Manal received his summons to the Military Prosecutor earlier today, while she was painting the new nursery. So, this morning, as I sit down to write, this is what's on my mind.

My family plays musical chairs with dwellings, and I find myself now, after four moves in thirty years, in possession of the flat in Zamalek where I grew up. When I lift my eyes from my desk – my mother's desk, her card still there, in the corner under the glass by my right hand – when I lift my eyes there's the view that used to meet them when I was studying for my university exams, and before that, for my finals at high school. The view is unchanged except for the 15 May Flyover that runs about a hundred metres to my left. Under it are the traffic lights at the intersection of Shagar el-Durr Street where in '67, and as the military were preparing for the war with Israel that they would lose with such catastrophic consequences, they crushed my uncle Khalu's Citroën between two massive trucks. So I stare out of the window and I think about civilians and the military and how Khalu, though he was an only son and so not conscripted, lost an eye, an arm and a career to them anyway and, in the end, was killed by an infection that entered his brain through an unhealed crack in the skull, a crack that happened in that accident twenty-eight years earlier. I think of Sally, my best friend, and how we sat in this room soon after we met on our first day at university, and she told me that her fiancé, her cousin, serving his conscription, had been captured by the Israelis in Sinai in the war. He was never heard of again.

I think about civilians and the military and how this year and within the revolution our army started, on 28 January, to grab and beat civilians, and to detain them and subject them to military trials. Six thousand two hundred and thirty-five young people are serving military

sentences now. Another twelve hundred and twenty-five
are carrying suspended sentences. The army picked up a
few here and a few there at every one of the 'incidents'
that have punctuated our lives since February, culminat-
ing, for the moment, in the events at the Israeli Embassy
on 9 September and the events at Maspero on 9 October.

On 11 February it seemed that we had emerged into
a clear open space and that our progress would be swift.
Now, eight months later, our landscape is more ambigu-
ous, more confused. I try to describe it and big, dramatic
clichés crowd into my head: the Forces of Darkness, the
Battle against Evil. But clichés can also be true descrip-
tions. Hosni Mubarak threatened that it was either him or
chaos. Not because that was the natural order of things, but
because if we chose not-him the forces that he represented
would work to create chaos. Mubarak and his family were
the packaging, the casing that held the Forces of Darkness
together, that utilised them, through his National Democratic Party, his security apparatus, his corrupt government
and the corrupt elite inserted into almost every leadership
position in the country. Now the casing's been smashed
and the Darkness is out there, unchannelled, panicked,
rampant, twisting into every nook and cranny as it seeks
to wrap around us again.

On 11 February, SCAF became de facto President, but
they kept in place the Cabinet appointed by the deposed
President, and on 26 February the Military Police attacked
protestors demanding its resignation. On this occasion
the army apologised – and appointed Essam Sharaf and
his Cabinet – but they had taken several young people
into military detention and a path was set. Not one step

or procedure that should have followed on automatically from the success of the revolution and the removal of the head of the regime was conceded without a struggle, without protests and demonstrations and sit-ins. And each one of these was punished more severely than the last.

The slow pace meant that the 'remnants' of the regime had time to collect themselves, to organise. Mubarak's sons were in jail but they still had their cash and their connections and their mobile phones. Zakareyya Azmi, Mubarak's Chief-of-Staff, lived a normal life after his boss fell, with daily access to his office for two months before he was arrested. Omar Suleiman, Mubarak's last-minute Vice-President and long-term Head of Intelligence, continues very much at large and is even being proposed by SCAF from time to time as a serious candidate for the presidency. If twenty corrupt politicians/businessmen are being tried, fifty more are still free. The decapitated regime is still strong, it's fighting for its life – and possibly growing a new head.

Its weapons have always been cash and coercion. For coercion it used its 1.5 million strong security apparatus – plus the estimated half million or so baltagis. The Minister of the Interior, Habib el-Adli, was arrested in February, but SCAF have allowed no one to examine, punish, rehabilitate the security establishment, so the country is full of armed and disgruntled police and baltagis, short of cash and ready to be used. The regime is still rich. And the old alliance between the regime and the security establishment is still in place.

And so we, the citizens, resort to the law courts and to direct action. Citizens file legal cases to place barri-

ers between the regime and its money; cases against
individuals, against companies, against transactions.
Citizens propose ways forward for employment, education, agriculture, the Dakhleyya; a few days ago a group
of professionals announced their detailed blueprint for
its restructuring and reform. Other citizens sue it for
murder, terrorism and torture. And the shabab periodi-
cally besiege it and spray graffiti portraits of the murdered
shuhada on its walls. Meanwhile, we have no effective
security and a sizeable number of our police force are
working with paid criminals – attempting to cause chaos
and disruption.

When SCAF promised to 'protect the revolution' we
assumed that this meant protect it against its declared
enemies: the Dakhleyya, the 'Remnants' of the old regime
and the influence of the outside forces that wished it ill;
that it would hold the state in place as we, the people,
went through the process of electing a parliament and a
president to whom SCAF could hand over power.

We assumed that SCAF would want a guarantee that
it would not itself be tried for corruption, and perhaps
would want an agreement about the position of the military in the future. This could have been something to
be negotiated. Quite soon, though, it became clear that
SCAF's policy was to conduct a war of attrition against the
revolution and the revolutionaries.

Why?

You, my reader, are better placed to answer this than
I. From where we are now we can only guess at where
they think they are leading us, and our dominant guess
is that SCAF want the old regime to continue, but with

some cosmetic changes, maybe completely new faces. They would prefer not to have to impose an overtly military dictatorship to do this. So they will let the elections for Parliament happen, but they will work – have been working – to ensure the elections do not deliver a 'revolutionary' parliament. Then they will insist that the Constitution is written before we elect a president. They will remain Acting President and will veto any real moves to change the system and deliver on the aims of the revolution. They will also intervene strongly in the writing of the Constitution – maybe to give the military a constitutional role overseeing a civilian government.

These are only guesses.

As I write now we are supposed to be heading for parliamentary elections on 28 November. But SCAF are talking of eighteen months before they hand over power to a civilian president, while all the political forces in the country (apart from the Remnants) insist that six months is their ceiling. Meanwhile, paid advertisements by Remnant MPs have appeared in the state press inviting SCAF to declare martial law.

The SCAF generals, and Field Marshal Tantawi, repeatedly inform us that they 'took a decision' not to shoot us during the revolution. Yet Tantawi has testified in court that Mubarak never gave him an order to shoot the revolutionaries. We know that the military conducted a poll among its field officers very early in the revolution and learned that officers would refuse a direct order to shoot at the people. We also know that the military were completely against the Mubarak plan to insert Gamal Mubarak into the presidency.

It seems, then, that SCAF discussed among themselves, of their own accord, whether to shoot us, and decided not to because they feared a mutiny in the army. In any case, we were getting rid of Gamal Mubarak. They didn't like to see Hosni Mubarak himself go down, but they've been making his fall as gentle as possible. And, meanwhile, they've been gradually getting their officers used to harming us.

Our story, since SCAF, with tanks in the streets, stepped forward and promised to protect our revolution, has been a story of SCAF impeding, delaying, blocking every practical aspect of the revolution; every possible step towards the goals of the revolution – while paying florid lip service to 'the Glorious Revolution of 25 January'. It has been a story of SCAF attempting to close down the public space so hard won by the people. And it has been a story of the people taking the revolution into the workplace: strikes and unionisation in factories and hospitals, strikes for elections and transparent budgets in universities – ports, banks, law courts, schools. Since there's no 'government of the revolution' making a plan that includes everybody, everybody's trying to act out some aspect of the revolution in their own sphere. And, whenever possible, SCAF has held up the process. Court judgements to return fraudulently sold national assets, needing presidential ratification, are left unsigned. Officials who negotiate deals with factory workers are fired. A law to prevent Remnants running for office for five years is blocked. And more and more and more.

And so it has been a story of escalating confrontation between the revolutionaries and SCAF. Instead of 'The

People! / The Army! / One Hand!' it's become 'Down! Down with the rule of the generals!'

The incidents that mark our progression down the route of confrontation over the past eight months can be generally grouped under the headings 'internal' and 'external'. The 'external' incidents focus on the Israeli issue. The 'internal' ones focus on division; and to the Mubarak agenda of dividing Muslim from Christian, Islamist from non-Islamist, Egyptian from non-Egyptian and rich from poor, SCAF have added people from the army. Even though it was the people's anger on behalf of the army that led them to protest in front of the Israeli Embassy on 20 August when Israeli forces killed three border guards in Egyptian Rafah and wounded three more – all of whom were to die of their wounds.

Protestors headed to the Israeli Embassy to demand an apology, the dismissal of the Ambassador and the lowering of the flag. Essam Sharaf's government did nothing except ask the Israelis for an explanation. The Israelis refused to apologise. The Israeli Embassy is on the sixteenth floor of a residential apartment block. At dawn on the 21st a young housepainter climbed to the sixteenth floor, took down the Israeli flag and raised the Egyptian. The crowds celebrated with fireworks and music.

This was not the first time the shabab had demonstrated in front of the Israeli Embassy.

Egypt had celebrated when Nabil el-Arabi – in his brief tenure as Minister of Foreign Affairs – opened the Rafah border and brokered a peace between the Palestinian Authority and Hamas. But a few days later, on Nakba

Day on 15 May, while people across the world marched
in support of the Palestinians, the Egyptian army stopped
Egyptian buses crossing into Sinai; SCAF would not allow
a peaceful march to Rafah. So the march went to the Israeli
Embassy – where it was attacked by the Egyptian Military
Police; young men were ordered to kneel on the road in
front of the embassy and to repeat the chants of Tahrir and
beaten while they did it. Many young men were taken
into military detention and one, Atef Yahya Ibrahim, was
shot in the head. He was twenty-two. He would remain
in a coma for five months – then die.

The symbolic victory won by 'Flagman' was quickly
dampened when Sharaf's government, in a brilliantly
obtuse move, built a grey fortified wall – reminiscent of
the Israeli apartheid wall – on University Bridge facing the
entrance to the embassy block.

Friday 9 September was designated to 'Realign the
Revolution'. After songs and speeches all day in Tahrir
the shabab marched to the symbols of the entities
they wanted 'realigned': the Supreme Court building,
the Dakhleyya, the Radio and Television building in
Maspero and the Israeli Embassy. The marches were
all peaceful and they were all to demand changes of
government policy. At the embassy they battered down
the brand new wall. Then several young men climbed
the building and brought down the new flag that had
replaced the Egyptian one. What happened next is still
under investigation. But what all the stories agree on is
that neither the army nor Central Security – and both
were present from the start – tried to stop the group that
went into the building and broke into the apartment

used by the embassy for storage. It was only after papers had been thrown out of the windows that the army and Central Security suddenly acted. They detained twenty-six people, injured 1,049 and killed three: Mustafa Hasan, twenty-four, Ala Salem, twenty-three, and Ragab Hussein, also twenty-three. Next day they came back and detained a further ninety-two people who happened to be in the area. All the detainees are being court martialled. In an effort to support them, twenty-one political groups have claimed responsibility for the 'embassy events'.

Our issues with Israel are issues of sovereignty and of running Egypt in Egyptian interests; both prime movers of the revolution. Until we have a government that we trust with our sovereignty and our interests the shabab will be again and again put in the position of protecting them. And this will be represented to the world as 'chaos' and 'irresponsibility'. And will be presented to the army as the shabab being careless of them; cavalier in pushing them into a new war. And a new wedge will be driven between the people and the army.

Consolidating this dangerous division, a new alliance is forming. The military and security establishments, long played against each other by Hosni Mubarak, are coming together. SCAF have refused any restructuring of the Dakhleyya; they cancelled the Central Security Forces and reappeared them as the 'Anti-Riot Police', and they renamed the State Security Service as the 'National Security Service'. This alliance embraces state media; the building in Maspero that was always protected by the Presidential Guard. And it uses and is used by the Remnants – whom

SCAF has refused point blank to remove from any field of public life.

And the tired tactics of the Mubarak era are very much in play: the attempts to sow division, to make people afraid of each other, of foreigners, of 'outside forces', of 'infiltrators'; the harping on the need for 'stability', the need to not frighten investors, to not 'sully' Egypt's image abroad, the need to respect the state and its instruments.

Security's fingerprints are familiar to us: find a fault line and wrench, spread rumours, use cash, insert *agents provocateurs* – and then attack. And we've been finding these fingerprints everywhere in the military's dealings with the revolutionaries. Looking through our diaries we agree that the tactical marriage of police and army began with the events of Abbaseyya on 23 July and consolidated in the period till the break-up of the Tahrir sit-in on 1 August.

23 July 2011

'This is the hospital where you were born,' my mother would say whenever we drove past it. And I'd be mildly annoyed. 'I know. You've been telling me since I was born.' As I grew older I made a joke of it. Sometimes I'd get in first: 'Mama, mama, what's this building?' She'd peer over her glasses, then frown at me: 'It's the hospital where you were born. And you're being silly.' My mother didn't much like being teased. Except by her grandchil-

dren. Well, now that she's no longer here to say it, I think
it. Always. At this junction. Always, always, always. This is
the hospital where I was born. Soon, I might start saying it
to my children. Maybe I already do. Now, I say it to Sherif
Boraie, the friend with whom I'm driving in pursuit of the
march: 'This is the hospital where I was born.'

The march left Tahrir at five, aiming to go through
the Abbaseyya neighbourhood to the Ministry of Defence
on the airport road. There we would hand in our list
of demands. Five months after our glorious, wonderful,
successful revolution, we continue to protest and hand in
demands – now to the Supreme Council of the Armed
Forces, our acting president. SCAF have been dragging
their feet on every issue we need to move quickly on: a
schedule for elections, cleaning up state radio and television, reforming the Dakhleyya. And they've been arresting
young people on any variety of charges and summarily
trying them in front of military courts. Today our demands
are a clear job description for SCAF and a detailed schedule for elections to Parliament and the presidency; we
want the police officers accused of murder and intimida-
tion by the families of the shuhada arrested; and we want
the court martialling of civilians to stop.

And we have the now standard paragraph demanding that SCAF and the Cabinet timetable a start on social
justice programmes such as minimum and maximum
wages, re-examining the budget, employment policies and
pensions and national insurance systems. We know they
won't do this; this will be the work of our elected government, but we have to keep the demands on the table. And
we have to make sure we get to elect a government.

A statement on Thursday counted the revolution's recent gains: the Cabinet reshuffle, the decision to hold the Mubarak trial openly and the decision to allocate courts to the trials of regime bosses and people accused of murdering the young revolutionaries – all of them wrenched from SCAF and the Cabinet through escalated protests and sit-ins.

Today's march was planned to coincide with the anniversary of the revolution of 1952; to remind SCAF of the celebratory phrase, the mantra everyone was repeating in February: 'In 1952 the army revolted and the people supported the revolution. In 2011 the people revolted and the army protected the revolution.'

The march left Tahrir at five but Sherif said he was driving in order to carry water and biscuits and stuff. Sherif is a publisher of exquisite books. Since the revolution began he's been the 'father' of a core group of activists; looking out for them, supporting them, and often underwriting their projects. I rode with him and we zigzagged through Downtown and arrived at the Gala2 junction to see our friends marching past us as we sat in the traffic jam. And facing me, across the march, is the Gala2 Hospital. It's the hospital where I was born.

He was twenty-six and she was twenty-three and I was their first child. They were living in Shubra and they were poor, because even though they had both graduated with distinctions they couldn't get proper jobs – and certainly not in their university, Cairo University, which was what they wanted more than anything. Except to be together. The university was not allowed to appoint my father because when he was nineteen he'd joined a Communist group and been jailed for a year. My mother had graduated from the English Department and you couldn't be appointed to the English Department unless you were English. Or at least British. So he had a clerical job in Fisheries and she taught at primary school. They were poor also because both their families had objected to the marriage, and even though the families had come round and were anxious to help the young couple the young couple would have none of it and insisted on living on their own resources. So, they rented a flat in Shubra at the very very end of civilisation and my father worked on his MA (*Al-usus al-nafseyya l-el-ibda3 al-fanni* – Psychological Factors in Artistic Creativity – which became a classic) and my mother on her stories (which sit, unfinished, in a cupboard in my living room) and they agreed they couldn't manage kids yet so they tried to abort me but I wouldn't let go; I hung on in there till we were over the first three months and my mother surrendered and knew she had to have me.

She had me on the trolley in the reception courtyard of the Gala2 Hospital fourteen months after they married. The doctor who admitted her looked and said, you have a long way to go, and she said no, the baby's coming. And out I came, in this hospital, at the mid-point between my mother's family home in Ataba and the flat in Zamalek that we were to move into seven years later.

Depending on the point my mother was making, this was a story about how I was always in a hurry. Or it was a story about how she always got things done in record time. She had me in an hour, and she had my sister in the middle of the Ph.D. that she finished in two and a half years. She wrote the last chapters pregnant with my brother, my sister levering herself up against her legs to toddle off into trouble. But that was in London and in another story.

Here, in the Cairo story, the 1952 revolution happens and the two young graduates are appointed to Cairo University, travel abroad to study further, and return to set up the main geographical axis of my Cairo life: Zamalek/Ataba, Ataba/Zamalek. A straight line across Abu el-Ela Bridge, through Boulac, past the wonderful ruins of the Khedivial Stables with the carved horses' heads, past the hospital where I was born, past the magnificent High Court, through Fouad Street with downtown unfurling on both sides of it, past Midan el-Opera and past the National Theatre and the Ruwei3i and into the passage under my grandfather's house – which is where my brother was born. Not in the passage – in the house, with Toufi looking after my sister and Khalu playing distractingly noisy games with me on the stairs till the doctor left and I went inside and found my mother in her pink chenille dressing gown with baby Ala in her arms. 'Each one of you was unwanted,' she would tell us, 'and the moment I held you in my arms – each one could not have been more beloved.'

And now the traffic has moved and we're driving through Ramses Street and past the Coptic Hospital until we're right behind the 3,000 or so people in the march; behind a boy in a lime-green T-shirt with a Dolce & Gabbana logo. I catch a glimpse of Mona, one hand holding a phone to her ear, the other distributing leaflets: 'No to Military Trials for Civilians'. Marches that went out in Alexandria and Suez on Thursday were fired on. There were arguments throughout yesterday and today about whether this march should go ahead – but the general feeling among the shabab was that we have to keep up the pressure on SCAF. So even those of us unsure about this particular march are here to support and to witness. In the street, we are back to the instigator chants: 'Why why why so quiet? All we want is your rights.' Again there are the people on the balconies, watching us, but now mostly impassive. The street tries to carry on with its life.

After the Cathedral and by Ein Shams University Hospital we park. We load bags with water bottles and join the march through Abbaseyya. We walk. Maybe 400 metres or so and suddenly we're concertinaing into the people ahead of us and the cry is coming from the front: 'El-Geish—' – the army has closed off the road. We're at a dead end. We all press forward anyway to see the army. At the bottom of the access road to the airport flyover the road is blocked off with thick coils of barbed wire and behind them there are three lines of Military Police, each man cradling a gun. Behind the men there are the tanks. To our right there are people's houses and one narrow lane passing between them. To our left the iron railings of al-Fat7 Mosque, then the grounds of the University Hospital – at the other end of which we'd parked. The mosque has closed its gates and a line of soldiers is deployed inside its railings. An imam is holding on to the gate and remonstrating ferociously with the soldiers. People say he's the imam of the mosque and has somehow been locked out. We've come to a stop but there's that seething milling about when a crowd can't get to where it wants to get. The shabab at the

front are nose to nose with the soldiers across the barbed
wire. It's a stand-off and we don't know what to do. I
think a lot of the shabab are actually willing, now, to take
on the army. But we won't let them. We chant: 'The
army's ours / The Council's not.'

This morning SCAF issued Statement Number 69.
They accused one of the most active movements of the
shabab, the 6 April Movement,[19] of 'special agendas' and
of trying to make trouble between the people and the
army. SCAF denied that the military used violence in Suez
or any other city, and urged 'The People' to confront this
'suspicious plot to destabilise Egypt . . . with all strength'.
And General Hasan al-Ruweini, the Commander of the
Central District, i.e. Cairo, who had just boasted that he'd
started several rumours in Tahrir during the eighteen days,
warned on TV that 'the people from Tahrir will be coming
into Abbaseyya from three directions armed with weapons
and Molotov cocktails'. So the citizens of Abbaseyya are
waiting for us, and they're expecting trouble, and because
the army has closed the road and we can't move forward
they fear that we will start a sit-in on their doorstep. They
stand in windows and on balconies watching us. We stand
in the streets and chant: 'Friends and neighbours / Abbaseyya / Our protest is selmeyya.' But the feeling around us
is not positive.

The first stones come from a group of men who've
emerged from beside the army line. Then they come
from balconies and roofs. The men on the roofs are in
string vests. We can't really look up because the stones are
flying at us. After the first shock, young men start to pick
up stones and hurl them back. At first some of us rush

up and disarm them: 'Selmeyya! Selmeyya!' we shout
again and again – but very soon, as the rain of stones gets
thicker and as the stones start to come from the side street
as well, it isn't possible to stop the shabab. A mother
holds on to her son who's trying to break free and run to
the front lines. He's about ten or eleven. Quickly we're
four adults holding him back: stay here and be a man.
Protect your mother! A car on the side street bursts into
flames. People retreat from their balconies and close their
shutters.

I watch our shabab surge towards the mouth of the
side street. Leaders try to stop them: defending our position on the main road is one thing; pursuing people
into a neighbourhood is another. The buildings are now
completely shuttered. All the fighting is in the side street,
and it rages on. The army stands behind its barbed wire,
cradling its guns and watching. Two young men run out
of the side street carrying a third with blood on his face.
They run past me, away from the army lines, about thirty
metres along, then lay the boy down by the side of the
road. Almost immediately a young woman bends over
him; a doctor. A stone lands by my feet. I pick it up. It's
not a stone but a chunk of thick ceramic tile. It's when
I hold it in my hand, feel its weight, its jagged edge,
that I suddenly feel what its impact would have been on
my head. I suddenly, for the first time, feel vulnerable;
recognise that I'm standing in the middle of the road
with tiles and stones hurtling round me. I start to move
but that seems worse, like I'll actually run into one of
them. I stop. I'm uncertain. Then I feel two hands take
hold of me, one presses my head down and the other

holds my arm above the elbow and propels me forward and I feel my speed double with the energy of the man who's pushing me to safety. I think this is like planes refuelling in midair. I stay under the tree where he's put me and watch the street. Sometimes I see Omar. Sometimes I see Alaa or Mona or Sherif or other friends. Laila is at the front near the army where a line of young men stand glaring at the soldiers, taunting them. Stones land and skitter on the asphalt. Young men run backwards and forwards carrying other young men and sometimes women. Sometimes a stone catches one of the young men and he staggers as he carries his wounded comrade to the makeshift emergency clinic at the side of the road. There are two doctors there now and a crowd around them, fanning the boys who lie on the ground, pouring water over them, trying to call in ambulances and medical supplies over the phone.

I sit on the kerb under the tree. I don't know what this is about. SCAF, officially meant to be preserving order and running the country – never mind protecting the revolution – what's their problem with receiving a set of demands? What would have been the worst thing we could do? Chant in front of the Ministry of Defence. Why the baltagis and the stones? Since when does the army use baltagis and stones? This is a disaster; people are getting hurt. And we're losing neighbourhood support. I grab Alaa for a second as he passes. He says we put out the car fire. They're telling us it's the army on the roofs, not the locals.

The mosque has opened its gates and the imam has gone inside. Sherif and other people come to my kerb. There's

talk of retreat, of pulling the shabab back from the side
street and marching together back to Tahrir. Then people
come running up from the rear: we're surrounded; there
are Central Security Forces and they're blocking the road
we came from. We all run down to look. Central Security
is meant to have been disbanded but here they are: the
black-uniformed phalanxes, the helmets, the visors, the
shields. And behind them the muscled toughs in civilian
clothes. I watch the first Molotov cocktail crash out from
behind their lines.

Word of the Central Security trap behind us has reached
the shabab facing the army. Their chants rise to a roar and
they grab the barbed wire and start shaking it. The soldiers
raise their guns and I run up so close that I can see the anger
in their eyes – anger and threat. I'm struck with fear for the
young men. I think the soldiers would like to shoot them,
then my sister steps forward out of nowhere, and with her
two older women, one with a hijab and one without. They
shove several young men out of the way and they're standing in front of the soldiers with their arms spread wide.
'Shoot us then,' they say to the soldiers, 'shoot the women.
Shoot the mothers of Egypt. Shoot your mothers.'

The shabab are running out of the side street and racing
down the road to face up to Central Security. It's gone dark.
Stones, stones and Molotovs and then the tear gas explodes
in the middle of the road. Alaa runs past me and I grab hold
of him again. I daren't speak to Omar, but I can speak to my
nephew: habibi, this is about nothing. Nothing. What's to
win? Sherif is checking a way through the hospital grounds.
We have to leave. We can't leave. But this isn't Tahrir; this
is about nothing. I know, he says. But we can't leave while

one person stays. It's OK. We're trying to collect people. I
don't believe him. I believe that it's become a point of prin-
ciple: if Central Security or the baltagis attack the shabab,
the shabab have to win. They can't afford to lose a battle.
But what if someone dies? What about the boys lying in the
road? What if one of them dies?

Sherif says stones are being pitched from inside the
hospital grounds; the baltagis are in there. The mosque's
loudspeaker bursts into life. The imam is pleading for peace.
He demands that the army protect the shabab from Central
Security and the baltagis, that they open a path for people
to leave. There's an ambulance now in the middle of the
road. One half of a young man is hanging out of it and
several young men are strewn on the ground by the wheels;
their comrades lean over them, fan them, stuff clothes under
their heads. The imam calls for prayers and miraculously all
is quiet for the duration of evening prayers. Then the gas
comes again. The imam pleads angrily through the loudspeaker with the army: open a path. Open a path for the
shabab. Let them pass in safety . . .

It's dark and the air is smoke and gas. From the army
side there's silence. From the Central Security side there's a
constant roar and flames and the pop of gas canisters. From
the mosque the exhortations continue. I'm sitting on the
ground by the ambulance. My scarf is over my nose and
mouth and I'm pulling in shallow burning breaths. I don't
know where anyone is. I can no longer open my eyes.

Omar has his arm round my shoulders and is rushing
me through the alley that's been opened by the mosque.
Inside the circle of his arm I run with my eyes closed.
What breath I have I use to curse. He conserves his.

9.00 p.m.

Back at the sit-in in Tahrir we're subdued and angry.

One of our friends is missing. His brother says he was taken by baltagis. Many people have been injured. Two are critical. One of them, Muhammad Muhsin Mustafa, a 23-year-old activist from Aswan, will die of his injuries on August 3.

Everyone swears the sit-in will continue. Everyone is coughing and exhausted. We know now that the Central Security Forces are back and the army is working with them and with the baltagis. On the news they're saying we went to Abbaseyya armed with Molotovs and attacked the army. The *10 P.M. Show* call me and down the phone I give an account of what happened.

11.00 p.m.

At home I find a mountain of laundry on the kitchen floor. Shukri, who used to be my mother's driver and right hand, and is now Sohair's, has brought down all the linen and towels and cushion covers from my mother's summer house on the coast. They need laundering. He's had the house sprayed against flying insects and checked the electricity and plumbing. Normally we do all this in late May and get the house ready for use. My mother used to go up and we'd all come and go till September. The laundry is in the middle of my floor. I put the first load into the

machine. I don't know if any of us will manage to go up
at all this summer.

Sunday 24 July

Rabab el-Mahdi phones with an initiative to pull together
all the 'revolutionary political forces' to cooperate for the
protests called for Friday the 29th; it's the only way we can
pressure SCAF. Rabab is a young academic and activist
and special in that she's liked and trusted by the Islamists despite not being one herself. Friday will be about
speaking with one voice, she says. And about time too, I
think. The leadership of the political forces are like cells
gone mad, they swim around frantically, they divide, they
coalesce with other cells then divide again, they accuse
each other of not being cells at all.

You could say that this is normal, healthy: people are
working out what they believe in and stand for – and
they're not used to working together politically because
anyone who tried to work together politically over the last
sixty years was destroyed. So the revolutionary forces are
really doing what they're meant to do and our society is
engaged in a process that will take time.

But we don't have time. Because the Remnants of the
old regime are gathering strength.

So, what do we want? We want to pressure SCAF for
a timetable for the elections. And we want everybody to
agree that the elections should be soon and for no one to

give SCAF any excuses to delay them, and measures put in place to ensure that they're free and fair. Meanwhile, we want to safeguard our world till the elections and to try to move on some procedures that would at least indicate that we're heading in the general direction of the revolution's goals. We could, for example, cut part of the fuel subsidy to the cement industry, bring down their profits to 50 per cent and use the seven billion annual saving to put in a 700 pounds a month minimum wage. I'm ashamed even to write down '700' when we know the real minimum wage should be 1,436 pounds a month. But there we are: this is a revolution that's chosen to work peaceably and legally – and it's paying a price for peace and legality.

But everyone absolutely has to speak with one voice. Rabab says she has the leaders from the Ikhwan, the Salafis and the Liberals. We have the Left and the Progressives. Everyone has agreed that Ibrahim al-Moallem of Shorouk should host it – because he has a lot of power and has maintained the same friendly distance from every faction. And that I should moderate – because I've no power at all and have no relationship with any faction.

I make lots of phone calls for this initiative. Our great problem, our maximum vulnerability, is the rooted, knotty, gnarled suspicion between the Liberal and the Islamist political currents.[20] The Liberals will remind you that the Ikhwan had declared in January that they would not join the revolution, that the Salafis held that rising against a ruler was a sin and they would live pure lives without touching politics. But that was the leadership. The shabab had all come together in Tahrir. Through the eighteen days Liberals, Progressives, Sala–

fis, Ikhwan, Leftists, Gama3at and those with no affiliation, just the desire for a better, cleaner, happier life, had rebelled together, broken bread together, talked to each other, slept in the same place, defended the Midan and, finally, died together – and they had discovered the vastness of the common ground they shared and the myriad meeting points between them and how much work they needed – and wanted – to do together. Many had begun to change, and to note and welcome the changes in themselves and others as they found this ground. But Mubarak fell and we all went home and the old leaders all started pulling their shabab back into line. Some couldn't go back and broke away – became, as it were, homeless in Tahrir. Some tried to form new groups, and some tried to form coalitions between groups and some stood alone and spoke truth. Everyone was madly busy. No one had control of anything.

But I make the many phone calls anyway and we set up the meeting for Tuesday.

And I manage to catch my younger son, Ismail, at home in London, for a few minutes on Skype and to make more inroads on the washing mountain before I fall asleep on the sofa, waking only when Omar comes home from Tahrir while the mosque is calling for dawn prayers. I stumble to bed and sleep till late. I think this is the aftermath of yesterday's events.

Monday 25 July

Monday morning at the Gezira Club with my father and my sister, as usual. Mr Muhammad Adel, one of my father's carers, has his right index finger in a big bandage. He is very ambitious and enterprising. His latest venture is a butcher's shop. He put his finger in the mincer and it cut off the tip.

My father is eighty-six. He still runs his research projects, his committees and his clinic and teaches once a week. He does this through having lots of support and being extremely organised. For the last decade he's also been writing monthly articles with titles like 'Psychological health in the absence of democracy'. The revolution has straightened his back and pumped up his voice. He is advising the activists of his college about the upcoming university elections. I think he is – in an out–of–the–self kind of way – living the happiest days of his life.

When he leaves Laila and I confer about the coalition meeting tomorrow.

3.00 p.m.

47 Ramses Street, to give a witness statement to TV channels about the events of Abbaseyya.

I meet the mother of military detainee Ahmad Gabir Mahmoud (detained and tried 3 February, ratified 9 February, moved to el-Wadi el-Gedeed prison 17 February). He was picked up from Hamad Mosque in Faisal Street, not in Tahrir. Accused of Molotov cocktails and breaking curfew. Sentenced to five years. He is nineteen years old. His friend, Muhammad Amin Gamal: same case, same treatment. They are both at secondary school, agriculture. 'They create criminal records for the shabab,' his mother says, 'they all had clean records before this. Now each one has a criminal record. Even sixteen-year-olds. Why are they doing this to us? I'm demanding justice for my son. We walked peaceably all the way from Tahrir to Abba-seyya to ask for justice. We broke nothing, we weren't disorderly. All I want is justice for my son.'

There are at least 8,000 mothers like her – and that's not counting the mothers of the martyrs, the shuhada . . .

The young woman speaking before I do is the tour guide who'd been detained in an armoured personnel carrier. The military found twelve dollars with her and accused her of being a foreign agent. They ripped off her hijab and beat and tasered her inside the truck and eventually said they would 'give her another chance' and let her go. She speaks very clearly and confidently. I cannot believe we are back to this.

All afternoon, phonecalls about the meeting tomorrow.

8.30 p.m.

Meeting in Simmonds Café with Mr Hasan Ali, Abu Muhab, the father of the shaheed, the martyr, Muhab Ali.[21] He has his daughter, Rahma, with him. She sits silently by her father giving me small, encouraging smiles when I look at her. They are the saddest smiles I have ever seen. Her brother was her best friend, two years older than her. She's just sat her school finals. She hasn't done very well. Yes, we all agree it would be best for both the revolution and the families of the shuhada if the Tahrir sit-in is suspended – not called off, just suspended. Everybody's tired and the weather's so hot and there's no progress and ordinary people are getting annoyed at the closure of the Midan to traffic. The calls to escalate the sit-in are worrying. Decisions are not taken collectively; every group has leaders but there's no joint leadership. But we need a strategy to suspend. The families won't leave with nothing. They're being harassed and they want the men, the officers, harassing them, the officers who killed their children, put away.

Abu Muhab and his son were together in Tahrir. They left when the army went into the streets because, he said, he'd lived through the bread riots in January '77 and didn't want his son exposed to the military. They went home and Muhab couldn't find his memory stick so he took his hard drive to go to a friend and download material. He'd changed into joggers and flip-flops and just popped out to his friend's. There was a small local protest on the traffic island at the top of the road and he joined it and there they shot him twice in the neck and he died.

Abu Muhab used to represent a pharmaceutical company. Since 28 January he has dedicated himself to Muhab and the revolution. He says he was responsible for Muhab's politicisation. I say we bring up our kids to do what's right. Beyond that I'm silent. I cannot – don't want to – imagine losing a son. He says: God has honoured Muhab with martyrdom and honoured me with being his father. He died for the revolution and I will live for the revolution.

Khaled Abd el-Hameed joins us. He's getting married
in a week – to a young Palestinian woman named 'Tahrir'!
He too wants to suspend the sit-in but he's worried about
suspending on a promise. At least let's try to get two conces-
sions on paper, he says. We look at yesterday's demands.
Abu Muhab gives me the names and stations of the officers
accused by the families: in Marg, Embaba, Alexandria and
Matareyya. Abu Muhab says his greatest sorrow is not for
his son, and not for all the martyrs; they live with God and
prosper. His sorrow is for what's to come. He says ninety
families have bought arms, and if they're not given satis-
faction soon, they will use them. They need something, he
says. He says I don't know who killed my son, but some of
them know who killed their children. And all of us know
who's still terrorising us and pressuring us; their names are
right here. Arrest these officers. Put them away for their
own safety pending trial.

I go home and hang out some more washing. More
phone calls. Alaa is on ONTV. Waleed Tahtawi phones
in to the programme. He's the brother of Ibrahim Tahtawi
who was killed on the 28th. And Hoda Tahtawi, who was
shot on the 28th and died yesterday. He says he wants to
understand why this is happening. Why his brother and
sister had to die. How the person who killed them lives
with himself. What he feels when he looks at his mother
knowing what he's done to other people's mothers. He
says he has received offers of money and death threats to
sign that his brother died of heart failure. He says he's had
to sleep away from home for the last ten days because of
the threats. He's being pressured to not submit his sister's
body for an autopsy. It's difficult enough to take the deci-

sion to have Hoda's body cut up – but to be threatened and offered bribes to go back on the decision is too cruel. The worst of it, he says, is not what happened to us, or what happened to the other families – the worst is what's to come.

Nahla Hetta calls me. Physician, activist, entrepreneur, she's a friend of Amr Helmy, the new Minister of Health whom Prime Minister Essam Sharaf has delegated to deal with the revolutionaries and the families. Amr Helmy is a 'people's choice'. She's just met with him and given him the list of demands. He's going to try and push for them over a Cabinet meeting scheduled for tomorrow and the day after. Then he'll meet her on Wednesday at five. She wants to take someone sensible from the shabab in Tahrir who will listen to what Helmy brings back from the meeting and whom we trust to tell him how good his results are and what more is needed. I am so tired, she says, what must we do?

Tuesday 26 July

Eleven a.m. meeting hosted by Ibrahim al-Moallem at Shorouk. We got everyone round a table and we've hammered out a deal to issue a joint statement on the aims and demands of the revolution. There will be joint organisation of Tahrir on Friday. The six officers that the shuhada's families want arrested will be outed in the Midan. No statement will be made now on the sit-in but they'll aim to suspend it – or at least open the Midan to traffic – from Saturday. The announcement will be made by the shuhada's families.

I wonder how many other groups are meeting like this. Trying to get people together; to push for unity. Tens. Hundreds maybe.

6. 00 p.m.

We have a draft – but our work is foundering on the phrase 'al-Irada al-Sha3beyya', The Will of the People. The Liberals are adamant that the phrase has been co-opted by the Islamists and they won't gather under it. The Ikhwan insist on it. The arguments get more and more detailed; they're to do with past experience and with what each group suspects of the other's intentions. The Liberals will not sign.

The committee coordinating on the ground seems happy working together despite the problems.

Where is all this tiredness coming from? Beyond seven o'clock I drag myself around like a wounded creature.

Wednesday 27 July

Nahla calls to tell me she's met Amr Helmy with a delegation of shuhada's and injured's families.

A Liberal friend phones and spends an hour telling me how the Islamists will double-cross us.

Abu Muhab calls and asks me to apologise to Nahla for the behaviour of the families in the meeting with the new minister. I call Nahla and she says they were concerned and upset but they'd behaved just fine. (In September Mona is to tweet about how the mother of a recently detained young man called her back to apologise if she'd been somewhat abrupt.)

Amal comes round with her tiny little baby, Amina. We put my mother's quilt on the living-room floor and play with Amina. My brother comes round and joins us on the floor.

I finish the last lot of laundry for the coast and send it off to be ironed.

Thursday 28 July

Wake up to a group email from Laila repeating her testimony about Amr el-Beheiri, the young protestor who was taken by the military in the small hours of 26 February minutes after she'd already saved him from them once. A military tribunal convicted him of possessing arms and sentenced him to five years.

Write and file my column. Use half of it for Laila's statement. Stay sitting at my mother's desk. I have cleared one drawer. The top left one. I cheated, because I just moved what was in it to the other drawers without looking. Now

I reach and open another drawer and there, lying on top of everything, is an old *London Review of Books* with two of Ian's poems. Two of my late husband's, Ian Hamilton's, poems. I close the drawer.

I make, and receive, many phone calls about tomorrow. Everyone says it's all under control. It's looking good. We'll all be out there and prove we can work together, just like in the eighteen days.

6.00 p.m.

Sohair drops by for tea.

The ironing man delivers the linen.

Shukri is driving Sohair to Alexandria tomorrow so he'll go to the coast and drop it off.

9.30 p.m.

Cannot carry on. Shower and get ready for bed.

10.00 p.m.

I can't go to bed without checking on the Midan.

10.30 p.m.

The shabab guarding the entrance are three lines deep. They are courteous and welcoming as ever as they check my ID, my bag. Women pat me down.

Omar is rigging up his screen as he's been doing at ten o'clock every night since the sit-in began. He has three street-kid helpers and a tea man has set up his stall near the screen. He and Khalid Abdalla, Tamer Said and Ziyad Hawwas (part of the Mosireen[22] Collective) have established 'Tahrir Cinema'[23] together with Lara Baladi. They've hand-built the large screen and borrowed equipment from home and family. Every night they show footage, clips, film from the revolution. From the first night it became clear that the material was new to a lot of people: Cairenes had not seen the films from the provinces, people from other cities visiting Tahrir had never seen footage of the action to take the Midan, or the vast protests sweeping into the centre from every part of the city. Within hours the cinema became an exchange point for material which volunteers quickly reproduced. Soon they were inviting guest curators to show their films or footage. A young Libyan came and showed a film. Tahrir Cinema was performing the function that the Egyptian state media had been too cowardly or too complicit to perform – even after 11 February. The cinema also helped stage TweetNadwa – the first non-virtual meetings of the Egyptian Twitter community.[24]

Now the big hand-made screen is up and people are starting to gather and sit on the mats. I go for a walk and to check things out.

And I find something is different. We've always had posters of the shuhada. Now there are also images of 'The Hated'. I stand and stare at posters of the Mubarak family, of their associates who became symbols of corruption, of the artists who stood against the revolution in its early days. And I think how the delay, the unwillingness of SCAF, the ineffectualness of the older leadership, the failure of the shabab to come forward as one coherent unit – are all conspiring to push the spirit of Tahrir away from the miraculous and into the mundane. But the tents are all there, in the central garden with the absent plinth in the middle of the Midan, each tent bravely displaying its banner and its exhausted revolutionaries. Even at this hour the weather is clammy and hot. People everywhere pick up conversations – mostly about what they think might happen tomorrow. I keep talking about unity and agreement and how all the 'patriotic forces' have agreed to work together. Any tentative mention of suspending the sit-in or moving the tents to the side is referred immediately to the shuhada families; Tahrir has centred itself on the killed and the wounded.

Omar's screen comes alive with the battle for Qasr el-Nil, the battle for Mansourah and some new footage from Suez. Then we see footage from Saturday, from

Abbaseyya. A young man in the audience tells how he
went back next day and people told him the men on the
roofs had been soldiers who'd taken off their uniforms,
and that baltagis and stones had been bused in from
the Wayli district close by. Hundreds of people are
watching; they sit on the ground, they stand in a great
semicircle. An activist from Qena says people there have
to see this material. Someone from Beheira says they need
to see it, too. State media is telling people the revolution's succeeded and everything is fine and on course and
needs to be left to the authorities. They're telling them
that anyone still in Tahrir, anyone who hasn't quietened
down and gone back to their pre-January lives, is a trai-
tor or a baltagi or misled and will cause the downfall of
the country. They're brainwashing people, they say, and
people have grown tired and want to believe them. So
the young cinemateers burn CDs on the spot and distribute them to whoever asks.

And as I write this it occurs to me that the shabab,
Omar and Tamer and Khalid, should have asked for donations, just one pound, whatever anyone could afford. The
suspicion that there was 'funding' for this revolution was
taking hold. As the regime was pushing the lie in January
and February, so SCAF and the state media are pushing it
now. We must be careful of looking as though we think
ten pounds is nothing.

I sit on the kerb with my sister and Ahmad Seif watching
the films. Ever since Omar and his friends set up this screen
I get a hint of that pleasant summer cinema feeling when I
come to Tahrir at night. One day, when the revolution is
safe, they can start showing the big classics. Revolutionary

still, but structured, and of a satisfying length. *The Battle of Algiers*, perhaps, and *Z*, and *el-Ard*. For tonight we watch the footage, and we also watch coaches arrive from the provinces. Each coach delivers thirty or forty men; mostly in shortened white thobs and white skullcaps, mostly with beards and no moustaches. Salafis. They walk in orderly lines, find sheltered spots on the peripheries of the Midan, and lie down and sleep.

Friday 29 July
Morning

Twitter is ablaze with news of Islamist banners going up then being taken down. And then with news of Salafi phalanxes hitting the Midan.

Rabab calls and says Salafist banners went up but the Ikhwan persuaded them to take them down. The joint organisation is working.

Rabab calls again and says I must not go into the Midan on my own; the Ikhwan say they can no longer control the banners or the slogans. 'Don't go in,' she warns, 'you may never come out. Come to Beano's by the American University; we're all there.'

A friend phones and says that the Salafis have been going round the villages in tok-toks telling people an important thing is happening in Tahrir and they're busing them in. ('Three pounds a ticket.' I hear next day, 'from any part of Egypt to Tahrir.') Whenever anyone describes people

as 'going around in tok-toks' I suspect them – perhaps
unfairly – of classism, because tok-toks are the transport of
the poor and the provincial.

I arrive at the Midan as Friday prayers are ending. I
catch the Prayers for the Absent. They feel different. I
can't quite put my finger on it but it all feels more down
to earth and practical. None of the emotion I'm used to in
the Tahrir Fridays.

I enter the Midan from Muhammad Mahmoud Street
– passing Beano's but electing to throw myself into the
Midan and see what happens. I do not need protection to
be in Tahrir.

Well, the crowding is like nothing I've ever been
through before. In the fullest days of the Midan when a
woman needed to move through the crowd there were
always men who miraculously formed a human cordon
that created a passage for her. Or there were lines of
people on the move and you took your place among
them. Here it's like some terrible crush at a bus stop. A
heaving and surging without getting anywhere. People
behind trying to push past you. Men, it's true, try not to
push you and try not to touch you, but it's hopeless. I
am hemmed in with the crowd behind the platform on
which Sheikh Safwat Hegazi is speaking. He stands on
the massive stage with his mouth to a dozen microphones
and one minute he's shouting: 'Muslim / Christian /
One Hand,' and the next minute he's shouting: 'Lift
your head up high / You're a Muslim.' The crowd
surges this way and that trying to move from behind the
platform. Street traders who'd pulled up their stands for
prayer time are pushing them out again – against the mass

of people, penning us against the platform. Men on the
stage throw bottles of water into the crowd, but throw
them so high and so far that I am sure you'd be hurt
if you were hit by one. One just misses my head and
I cry out. Sheikh Safwat is screaming into the microphones; he praises the army and SCAF. I remember
reading somewhere that in these crowd situations you
should stop trying to walk; just make sure you don't sink
and get trampled. Allow yourself to be carried by the
crowd. I try. I had thrown a scarf over my head during
prayers and now it's been dragged off and is throttling
me and I can't raise my arms to loosen it from my neck
or drag it back on to my head. Sheikh Safwat is yelling
in great triumph that iftar on 5 Ramadan, next Friday,
will be in the Midan: 'We shall break our fast in Tahrir!
We shall pray the Tarawee7 in Tahrir!' He is practically
sobbing with emotion: 'Then they'll know who we are!'
I don't understand what enemy territory he's capturing.
People have always broken fast in Tahrir. Tarawee7 have
always been prayed in Tahrir. Omar Makram Mosque, in
the heart of Tahrir, is the funeral mosque of choice for
Cairo. It's not like he's taking the believers to Jerusalem.
To be fair the crowd is not responding to his decibels
with corresponding enthusiasm. And there, I've got it,
the difference that's been eluding me between this Friday
and all the others: it's as though these hundreds of thousands in Tahrir today are – kind of – tourists. I don't feel
an energy coming from them, a wish to make something
happen. Their purpose is to be here and here they are.
I feel their bodies pushing against me but not their will.
But I see the Saudi flag flying in Midan el-Tahrir.

The knot of the crowd that I am in gets beyond the stage and I shove and shoulder and elbow my way out of the crowd and out of the Midan and into the mouth of Tahrir Street. It's still massively crowded but there's room to walk of your own volition. Groups of men and families wander along the street. Many, many of the men are in the white thob and the white skullcap and the beard-but-no-moustache. I walk towards Midan Bab el-Louq. For the first time ever I walk down this street and forget to even think about drinking a glass of carob juice at the shop on the corner. We used to come specially. Park and honk and the guy would come out with the big glasses of light red-black liquid on a tray. Now I walk past the entrance to his shop and the street of the Mosque of the Servants of the Compassionate in a semi-daze. Groups of people, mostly men, are drifting along the street, looking around like they've never been here before. I remind myself that this is their capital as well as mine. My back hurts. I find a raised shop doorway and sit down. I might as well be in an alien city. Groups are making themselves comfortable on the pavements. They spread newspapers on the ground and serve food on them out of plastic bags. What conversations I hear are not political at all: he said, she said, money, family, detailed, personal . . . I lean against the shop window and wonder if somebody will ask me to leave.

My younger son rescues me; Ismail phones me from London and says, where are you exactly? What's it like?

It's their country too, I say. I'm saved. I get up and dust myself down and describe it all to him as I walk away.

I walk to Sherif's place. He makes me tea and we sit silently in his air-conditioned study staring out at Midan Abdeen.

2.00 p.m.

Nahla Hetta calls. Can I meet her in Amr Helmy's office now?

I walk up to the Ministry of Health. He says there's been a decision that the Midan must be opened; the sit-in has to end.

Nahla and I tell him the shabab want to suspend but they won't abandon the shuhada's families. The families are exhausted but they say they're still being pressured and threatened to make them change their testimonies and drop their cases.

He says he's allocated Agouza Hospital to receive the injured and he will put a wing there at the disposal of the families; if they suspend the sit-in they can stay there. We say they really need to see some officers taken off the streets. We have their names.

He says this is serious: SCAF is determined to clear the Midan.

He also says he's looking for a young, revolutionary doctor to be in charge of the injured and the families at Agouza. I put him in touch with Hoda Yousri, a young doctor I'd met in Tahrir the night Mubarak didn't leave.

3.00 p.m.

Nahla's car smells of mangoes. It's just brought back a crop
from their farm. Which reminds me that I have to go and
collect our fruit as well, from my mother's little orchard,
and check on the repairs to the roof. I should really go
before Ramadan starts.

We sit in Café Riche just off the Midan. Sooner or
later everybody stops by Café Riche. At a long table
in a side room I see my brother and Ahmad Seif in a
meeting with their Initiative to Restructure the Security
System. Judge Ashraf al-Baroudi, the revolution's favourite for Minister of the Interior, is with them. Omar is at
another table with his group and Sherif at yet another.
Today Tahrir is operating out of Café Riche. Nahla and
I have meetings with several people about the conditions
for suspending the sit-in, or, a compromise suggestion is
to move the tents of activists who want to stay and place
them by the Mugamma3 near the tents of the shuhada's
families. To consolidate and tighten the sit-in, vacate
the central garden and allow the Midan to open. Most
people accept that three weeks is long enough to close
down the central midan of the third largest city in the
world, and that they need to take account of the residents
and business owners and shopkeepers of the area who're
getting fed up. This compromise would allow the physical manifestation of solidarity with the shuhada's families
to continue, keep a symbolic presence in the Midan and
undermine the theory – fast becoming popular – that the
Tahrir sit-in is responsible for all our ills, from the Cairo
traffic jams to the state of the economy. At four o'clock

we seem to have reached agreement and we write a draft announcement. Abu Muhab goes to have a final word with the families. We alert the newspapers and phone ONTV, al-Jazeera and al-Nil. Their crews arrive and set up. Abu Muhab does not come back. We phone him and he says they're still in discussion. Time passes.

At six the Salafis pack up and get into their coaches. We're back in possession of Tahrir. Some shabab put on plastic gloves and start collecting the mountains of litter left behind. We find Abu Muhab in the families' encampment near the Mugamma3. There are no lights. People are standing in clusters, arguing, shouting. Abu Muhab holds my arm, steadies me: it's dark and hot and the ground is treacherous. Judge Baroudi appears and begs everyone to understand the importance of unity, of working together. They listen then resume arguing. Strong voices argue for suspending. Strong voices retort that the closure of the Midan is the only card they have. I think people don't want to go home and pretend their lives are normal when their kids are dead. They need to remain in an 'exceptional' state. A woman faints. A young man on crutches tells me he's one of the 'injured'. He says they're offering him 10,000 pounds. And what happens to me when they're finished? he asks. I don't want money. I want a job. Abu Muhab gives me a folded sheet of paper. It's the draft announcement. Rejected. I phone the TV crews; we don't have an agreement.

Sunday 31 July

I steal three hours to go to the orchard. Osta Ashraf has laid palm branches down for the section of ceiling that's collapsed. I climb on to the roof to see his work from above. He urges me to walk on the branches, to jump up and down; the branches, he tells me, are stronger than steel. We're not using a teaspoon of cement in this work. It is so pure, so peaceful, up here that I don't want to come down. If I angle myself I see nothing except a sea of palm trees. And just beyond them, the Pyramids.

When I leave I'm loaded with mangoes, limes, mulukheyya and mint.

Monday 1 August/1 Ramadan

I see the tweets at about one o'clock: 'Tanks moving into Bab el-Louq. Must be heading for Tahrir.'
   'We have to open the Midan.'
   'We have to open the Midan now.'
   I phone Sherif. He's seen the armoured personnel carriers rolling out of Abdeen and is on his way.
   I get to Qasr el-Nil Bridge and run into the battalion arriving to control its mouth into Tahrir. They're maybe fifty men. They feel like army – tall and well-built and disciplined – rather than police or Central Security, but they're in black. They're carrying long

rough wooden sticks. They're almost forcing cars to drive through Tahrir; they bang on cars that want to turn right at the end of the bridge and push them towards Tahrir – until a boss soldier says to let cars turn right if they want.

The Midan is a massive wreck, a giant tip. They've demolished our small city. Abbaseyya was the first cooperation between the military, the Dakhleyya and the baltagis. Today is the try out for the Anti-Riot Troops, the new name for Central Security.

On Saturday, in the burning midday sun, Nahla and I and Abu Muhab stood with ten young people, at an impasse, between the Midan and Amr Helmy's office in Parliament Street. The shabab said we can't leave as long as some families and some activists won't go; we can't abandon them.

So don't abandon them; move your tents closer to them and open the Midan.

They wanted to but said there were a few who took a hard line and insisted that the closure should continue.

Who are these few? Can we talk to them?

They were mainly independents; and they'd become responsible for manning the accesses to the Midan. Some were young activists who'd worked on various campaigns for months; others were new but had worked hard and contributed to protecting the Midan for the last three weeks.

Please would some of you, or, better still, the hardliners, come and talk directly to Amr Helmy?

They said that for the hardliners even that would be treachery. Please help us maintain unity, they begged.

On Sunday we continued our failed shuttle diplomacy, crowning it with three unprofitable hours with the Deputy Public Prosecutor.

Now the Midan is overrun with soldiers. It's like a scene in a film when an army's been through an enemy village: everything's razed to the ground; the military pass through and the tents, the flags, the banners, the billboards – everything is transformed into rubbish. Military and Central Security (or, now, Anti-Riot) soldiers are on the move everywhere. Some civilians try to reason or object, some of the families try to go back to their positions, some of the passers-by make a point of showing support for the soldiers. We see young men being pushed by soldiers towards tanks, and we see soldiers deliberately breaking up unresisting chairs and tables. Some of the 'hardliners' who'd stopped the shabab opening the Midan are wearing the vests and headgear of the military over their civvies and chatting comfortably with the soldiers.

The Tahrir Cinema screen is on the ground, broken up by our army, the cables cut and tangled. I see the screen on the ground, then I see a child dragging a blanket behind him and crying. Then I see other children – children for whom the Midan had brokered a truce with their cruel lives and who'd found shelter in the central garden between the tents; the revolutionary shabab had held classes for anyone who wanted to learn to read or write, shared their food with them and given them responsibilities: the children spread mats and connected wires and held lights and cameras. All this in ruins now.

I spot Mona and Sherif and other friends on the
Hardee's corner and join them. They've just got news
of several activists detained by the military. We call our
human rights lawyer friends and report what we've seen.
A loud voice demands: who are these people? Are they
Egyptian? Why are they using their phones? There's
something theatrical about the voice, but the atmosphere
is suddenly tense. Mona says of course we're Egyptian.
'What are they doing?' voices shout. 'Let's see the
phones.' 'Mind your own business. Move away,' Mona,
Nazli and others are shouting back. We're actually scuf-
fling, or being scuffled; somehow we're in a crowd, we're
being pushed with shoulders and chests, we're pushing
back. A man looks at me and shouts: 'What's this one?
Look what she looks like!' I'm taken by surprise. 'Me?'
I ask. 'Yes, you. I heard you insulting.' 'Insulting who?
Tell me who did I insult?' I'm shouting at the top of
my voice but it's not carrying as I thought it would. I
do it again, above the jostling and pushing and yelling:
'Who did I insult?' His eyes flicker then he stares straight
at me: 'I heard you insult the Egyptian people. Yes,
you. I'm here and I'm a witness against you—' Focus
narrows right down: I don't know, see, hear anything
that's happening around me, it's just me and him: 'Me? I
insulted the Egyptian people, you son of a . . .' I hear my
voice yelling and swearing and I think I lunge at him.
Then there's a military chest in my face and a body of
soldiers between us and the crowd and the military are
hurrying us out of the square 'for our own good' while
we remonstrate: but did you hear what they said? Did
you hear—

They pushed us gently. Gently out of the Midan. But next day, when the families tried – not to camp, but just to break their Ramadan fast in the Midan, they were not so gentle.

Tuesday 2 August
Midnight

At Agouza Hospital taking the testimony of Mustafa Mursi, sixty-two, veteran of the Egyptian army, father of the shaheed Muhammad Mursi, shot and killed in Marg.[25]

Mustafa Mursi is on a hospital trolley. His shirt is bloody. He refuses to take it off and says he will return to Tahrir wearing it. He is accompanied by others from the shuhada's families. They confirm he was beaten by the army earlier tonight just after iftar.

Mr Mursi has a cracked rib and collarbone and bruises to the head and legs, and dizziness. He is diabetic, suffers shortage of breath and has shrapnel in his leg from service in the 1973 war. He speaks clearly but with frequent stops to catch his breath. He holds up the photograph of his son throughout the testimony.

I said [to the officer] we're going home, son. I was army too and I fought in '73. Swearing and cursing all of them. [Hitting me] on my head and on my chest till I collapsed. They took my son's photo from my chest and threw it on the ground and trod on it. I know them, the two officers. Army. One in camouflage, one in plain. I'll hunt them down. God willing. And I'll hunt down those who killed my son.

I was just saying to them that I am a man who – I am a man – I – my son. My son is now with the Just who never treats anyone unfairly. God forbade Himself injustice. He forbade Himself injustice but the rulers of Egypt and the corrupt regime in Egypt is unjust. But God is with the downtrodden. I want to follow my son because he's with the Just. Up there. Here, in the world of Egypt, there's no respect for humanity, or for age. The revolution came to clean the land of Egypt. But we still have a corrupt regime. Field Marshal Tantawi – we pray that God forgives him. We pray that God may guide him to the right path. If they wanted to control the situation two words would do it: arrest the officers who killed our children, and the snipers, and try them. Egypt would straighten out and the wheel would turn again. But they don't want to. Why? Because there's something in their hearts. Truly. I wish each one of them would sit with his conscience and with God and look into his heart. I hope they do it for the common good.

My heart won't cool until the people who killed our children are arrested. I'm not asking for any of that stuff – they're saying we'll give them this and that. What we have is enough. We lived under injustice and never harmed anyone and what God sent us was enough. But you see murderers and bribe-takers – my son, God knows, before he met God he knew Him well. He knew God. He's in the third year, Information Systems. His name is Muhammad Mustafa Muhammad Mursi. The Marg officers killed him and smashed his head. I'm over sixty now and we've never harmed anyone. God knows I speak the truth. All we want is that the officers who killed our children are arrested.

The army took me by treachery. I was going home. General Ruweini, when we met him he said we'll stand by you, yes stay in your tents, and we'd just arrived at our pavement and the army came and beat us and pulled down the tents on top of the shuhada's mothers who were preparing food to break the fast. They beat me with such cruelty and such stupidity that I got dizzy and fell. My chest is cracked from how hard they hit me. But God is present. God is here. With us.

October 2011 again

For weeks through August Central Security Forces occupied the central garden of the Midan. And in September we found out that the regime had been planning to sell Tahrir. They'd been planning to sell the central public space in our capital to a hotel chain, to a foreign hotel chain, because 'Hosni Mubarak's government was worried about large gatherings and protests . . . in central Cairo'.[26]

I'm not surprised because we knew that everything was up for sale: land, monuments, islands, lakes, beaches, people's homes, antiquities, stretches of Nile, natural resources, people, sovereignty, national parks, human organs, goldmines, the wealth under the ground, the water in the river, the labour of the people – everything.

And yet, every time we come across a specific transaction, a specific target, we're gripped again by that surprised horror: they would sell *what*? And it's no use saying well but we knew they were venal beyond venality, treacherous beyond treachery – you still feel your heart thump, and the pain in your stomach and the shiver down your spine: they were going to sell *Tahrir*?

But they would do anything . . . one never really believes that though; but they would, yes they would. What could be worse than trying to provoke conflict, war, within the community? That's what the regime has been doing between Muslims and Christians for more than thirty years. And that's what we detect again in what happened in Maspero.

If I had been in Cairo I would have been on that march on 9 October when thousands of Egyptian Christians and their Muslim supporters demanded the long-awaited 'Unified Law for Houses of Worship'. But I was in London and I sat watching it on fragmented screens: setting off from Shubra, walking, chanting, the people within it, old and young, talking even laughing. I felt the tension as it drew close to Maspero and then the great explosion of energy and noise and movement: the shooting, the armoured personnel carriers zigzagging among the people, hitting them, running them over, dragging them along. I heard the anchor of Channel 25 screaming as the channel was attacked while state TV tried to incite Muslim viewers with reports of soldiers killed and 'Christians attacking the Egyptian army'. Twenty-one civilians were killed that night, rising to twenty-eight later. And 1,400 wounded.

At my kitchen table I followed Alaa's heartbroken tweets from the morgue: 'Mina's body is here Mina my comrade I can't believe it', 'We lost you as you fought for our country may your soul be safe Mina Daniel my friend', 'I went in and saw them 17 pure bodies and Mina shining in their midst how shall we ever forgive ourselves'. But what Alaa and the shabab then did was remarkable; from the morgue of the Coptic Hospital they took on the entire system: in the face of the priests pushing for a speedy burial and the hospital administration issuing death certificates from 'natural causes' they persuaded the stricken families of the shuhada to demand their children's bodies be cut open. Activist lawyers pressured the Public Prosecutor to order autopsies. They fetched – bodily – the Coroner and his staff and persuaded them to carry out the autopsies in the presence of physicians – like Mona Mina – whom they trusted. And then they made them sit individually with the families and read and explain the reports to them. The hospital morgue only had three drawers so all the while they treated the bodies of their comrades with ice and fans, and they treated the anger, grief and suspicion of the families with tears and embraces and explanations.

Back in Cairo I went to visit the wounded at the Coptic Hospital – and they told me again about Alaa and his friends, Mina's Muslim comrades, who made sure the Christian shuhada were not hastily buried with their blood unaccounted for.

And now Alaa is summoned by the Military Prosecutor to answer charges of 'Incitement and Destruction'.

I can hear Omar on the phone at the other end of the flat, on the balcony where my nanny, who could not read or write, told me stories and gave me lessons in narrative. It used to amuse me that Omar would be working there on a script. These days he works on material for the independent cinema he and his friends at Mosireen are planning to set up – but right now he and Mona are working to put everything to do with the 'No to Military Trials for Civilians' campaign on one website.[27] Back in February, Mona created and spearheaded this campaign, and now she and Omar have their heads together over its papers like they used to have them over summer plans when they were younger.

Mona was always the good child; the one who laid the table and helped the smaller children. As a young scientist over the last year we watched her care for her – 'genes'? The things she was growing in the lab that she had to check on every three hours. Serious in her white coat and her spectacles, her hair bunched up, her earrings a gentle, time-keeping pendulum. And then there she was in the revolution – her effervescence stilled into seriousness. And now she peers into her laptop and answers her phone and the campaign in hand now is for her brother when he comes back from San Francisco. Our children.

For twenty years it was school year in England and holidays in Egypt. We would come back and all the children would fall in together as though they'd never been apart. I built a 'diwan' in the playroom, a wide bench that ran the four metres from wall to wall with a window behind it. I furnished it with a giant mattress and bright cushions and they all gathered on it to talk and play and watch movies and eventually fall asleep in a tangle like a litter of kittens. They ran together in Ataba, in Zamalek, at my brother's and my mother's and the little orchard and the house on the coast. And the first question every grown-up arriving at one of the houses asked would be: 'Where are the shabab?' Toufi fed them and embroidered their initials onto their school uniforms, my mother gave them books and listened to them, Lulie treated their cuts and colds, Laila helped with science and maths, Sohair was their confidante and my brother and Ahmad Seif were the still reference points who made everything special by their presence. And every child had their personality and their role. Alaa was the Guru who had a detailed and passionate opinion about everything. Omar Robert was the Lord of Games and quizzes and mischief. Mona was the Good Child and the Romantic. Salma was the Organiser, the one who bought tickets and got the family to things on time. Mariam was the Princess, born to be served. Ismail Richard was the Healer; a smile or hug from him made the world your friend again. And Sana was the Dreamer whose off-the-wall comments became family lore. And now they're all working for the revolution. And tonight Mona and Omar are preparing the campaign for Alaa and the newspaper on their table headlines a statement by the Chief Judge of the Military Judiciary: 'It is illegal to demand that civilians not be tried in military courts.'

What is legal and what is not? The Supreme Council of the Armed Forces, SCAF, makes up the rules as it goes along. The right to protest is enshrined in law, they say. But protestors in front of the Israeli Embassy are brutalised and hauled off to military trial. And every one of the incidents that have marked the last eight months has registered a worsening of the relationship between the people and the army.

The big question for us now – the question to which you know the answer and I don't – is will we have the parliamentary elections scheduled for 28 November? Many of us think the Maspero event was meant to cause enough civil unrest to give SCAF an excuse to declare martial law and postpone elections. It didn't work because Muslims did not respond to the incitement from state radio and television. Will it work next time? Will there be a next time?

'Not one of us is going to step back into the nightmare,' I wrote eight months ago. But the nightmare chases us, surprises us, attacks us. So far we have beaten it back.

And the thought is starting to take hold that maybe even elections will not lead to where we want to go. We are not alone. We were never alone; the feelings, the prayers, the messages that came pouring into Egypt from every place on earth during those eighteen days of Tahrir lodged in our minds and in our hearts and affirmed every minute what we knew already: that the freedom we sought was the freedom the people of the world wanted, for us and for themselves. And what has been happening across the planet since has confirmed and reconfirmed our belief. The first placards raised in Wisconsin, the street signs invented for the City of London, the words we hear from Tokyo to Wall Street, the chants in Oakland, California – all echo the call from Tahrir and Tunis: the people demand the fall of this – entire – regime.

THE EIGHTEEN DAYS RESUMED

1 February–12 February 2011

Central
CAIRO

250 yards

250 metres

6 october bridge

MASPERO

Myover

ELGYPTIAN
MUSEUM

FIELD
HOSPITAL

Corniche

TAHRIR
CINEMA

ARAB
LEAGUE

ANDALUS
GARDENS

gasr el nil bridge

OMAR
MAKRAM

MOGAMMA

gasr el nin street

paz

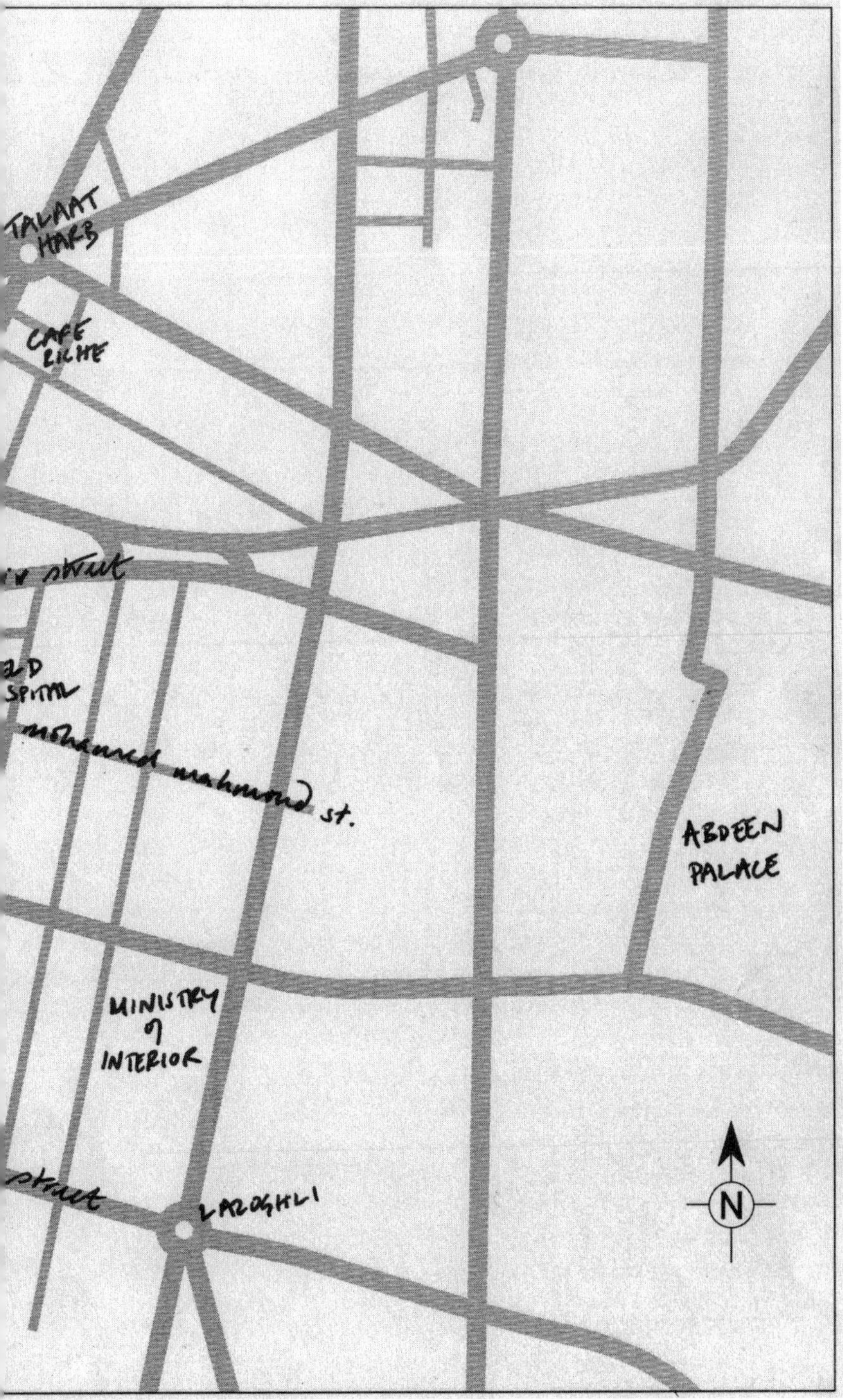
TALAAT HARB
CAFE RICHE
street
mohamed mahmoud st.
ABDEEN PALACE
MINISTRY of INTERIOR
street
LAZOGHLI
N

Tuesday 1 February
Evening

It's getting cold. But there's been an announcement that Mubarak will speak. We're hoping that he'll resign, and everyone wants to celebrate with everyone else when it happens. So we stay. We talk and walk and discuss and chant and shiver. They say he'll speak at 10.00, then 10.15, but it's 11.00 when he starts. There's no screen but loud-speakers are rigged up to lamp posts and everyone quietens for the address to the people. And we cannot believe what we hear. Hosni Mubarak has simply not understood what has happened. He talks of how some decent young people have been led astray and are being used by unnamed 'political forces', of how we're 'living together through these painful days'. He's suddenly aware of everything that's wrong and pretends that his regime which has been de-developing Egypt for thirty years and stealing the bread from our mouths is now suddenly equipped to 'respond to the demands of our young people'. He's going to create jobs and respect the law and run clean elections and put the police at our service and all he wants is a chance to end with honour his service to his country. The second he finishes the call rises stronger and more determined than ever: 'Irhal! Irhal!'

2.00 a.m.

I want my mother. I am cold and shivery and I. Want. My. Mother. I cannot tell you how many people in the Midan have said to me, can you imagine if your mother were alive today? How she would have enjoyed this? I want to ring the doorbell, find her in the living room surrounded by newspapers with the television on loud. I'll turn it down, get some food from the kitchen and sit beside her and tell her everything that's happened. I want her to be astonished and amazed and indignant and tickled. I want her to interrupt and interject and laugh and question. I want to talk to her and I want to see her face.

Every night as I've left the Midan, I've thought for a moment I was on my way to see her.

Many years ago, with her living in Cairo and me living in London and the telephone an open line between us, I realised that things I did, or things that happened, never became completely real to me until I had told them to her; until she knew them too. And I so want her reality imprimatur, her seal, on everything that's happening, everything we're doing now.

Her last summer, 2007, I was sorting out her library while she lay on the sofa watching me, facing the French windows on to the balcony. And at one point I glanced at her and she had this curious expression, like in a movie when people see a UFO. And I went over and took her shoulder: Mama, mama? What is it? And she kind of shook herself and came back to me and she said, wonderingly, 'Do you know? I thought I saw a massive storm rolling towards us.' She paused. 'I'm worried about el-balad'; the country, Egypt.

My mother had always had solutions. She always knew what people should do better than they knew it themselves – and told them so. But she was stumped by our condition.

She was worried. And I was worried for her. Ever since I can remember I've been terrified at the thought of the world without her. That summer she seemed different, less combative, gentler. She'd had a problem walking for a few years. And I think she decided it wasn't going to get better. And she was – loosening her hold. I asked her not to. I really did. And she said gently so should I be an old lady in a chair for ever? And I said yes. Yes. You've always done things for us, not for you. Do this for us. And she laughed and said OK OK, don't fuss. But I worried. I made her have a brain scan. I was utterly surprised when she submitted. It came out fine. I arranged for an old friend of hers, a psychiatrist, to come and visit. She was vivid and happy and I'd swear there was a moment when they were flirting. But then they were both quiet and after a bit he said, 'What is it you're worried about? Are you worried about Mustafa [my father, who'd just been ill]?' She said no, he has excellent care – and we're all there for him. 'Are you worried about yourself?' No, my children and grandchildren are all around me. 'What then?' I'm worried, she said, about el-balad.

When she was six months pregnant with me, her mother told my father he had to make her walk a kilometre every day. The church of St Thérèsè, la Rose de Lisieux, was half a kilometre from their home in Shubra. So every evening my mother and my father walked to St Thérèsè and back. She told me this when, many years later, my car broke down in front of the church and I came back amazed at the hundreds of little notices of thanks, the gifts that had been left for the saint by Muslims and Christians whom she'd healed. There was even one from my favourite singer, Abd el-Haleem. So that summer, when I had to go to Shubra to buy a noticeboard, I went into St Thérèsè and said a little prayer.

But my mother slipped away one night while I was in London. All it took her was fifteen minutes.

Just two weeks earlier I'd seen her and my two boys sharing the massive diwan in the living room, and Omar was reading to her, for a treat, her choice of poem. It was a toss-up between Pope and Byron, but she went for Pope. I used to be unable to gaze full on at that image of her laughing and repeating choice phrases. Now, for some reason, I can do it. These days I see her constantly, looking surprised, looking delighted, looking up every time one of us walks into the room: What's the news? Fein el-shabab? Where are the young people? What are they doing? And I tell her: Mama, you would be so proud of them; of your grandchildren, and of your students and the children of your students. Of all our young people. They are out there: and they are so many.

Wednesday 2 February

Aches and shivers. Sore ear, nose and throat passage, and those nightmare suites of consecutive sneezes where you don't have a second to gasp for breath. By the time nine sneezes in crescendo have pumped the air out of me I am collapsed on a chair in the hall, glad to be told to stay at home and do 'media work' rather than go to the Midan.

I knew something was wrong as soon as I woke up. There were car horns. It had been so quiet and peaceful for the last few days that we'd started to see the bats once again flitting in and out of the fruit trees at dusk. And this wasn't even the normal noise of Cairo traffic; this was aggressive, patterned and constant.

Out of my window I can see bands of people marching across 15 May Flyover and I realise, even before I see the banners, that these are the 'other lot', the pro-Mubaraks. My immediate thought is that they have a right to march. My second is that they're not actually freely expressing their opinion. They are regimented: each band of fifteen or twenty men (always men) accompanied by a honking car; even from this distance, they lack the civility, the friendliness of the protests: they carry sticks, they make provocative gestures at the street, they have obvious leaders, 'stewards' even, marshalling and directing them. The banners they carry are the uniform, professional banners we've grown used to seeing at election time.

Why am I taken by surprise? Because we need to believe that the whole country wants to get rid of the regime? Why am I disheartened? Because I thought the regime had vanished for ever after the 28th and now it looks like it will fight back – and on the streets, which should now belong to the revolution? Because I'm ill?

I am ill. Layers of jumpers, woolly socks and a hot-water bottle to hug. Boxes of tissues. But it doesn't feel right to just lie down and take it easy; we all have to be useful. The novel I've been working on (and off) for the last several years has gathered itself into a cold little knot in the corner of my mind: is my novel obsolete? My characters, discussing the state of Egypt, the state of the world, acting, working, loving – are they dead? If I think about it I'll be racked with guilt and self-blame that I did not finish it two, one, half a year ago, when I could have, and then it would have been part of what's happening now, it would have been part of the great turmoil of ideas and discussions that are taking place. But no-o-o-o, no: I procrastinated. I did a million other things when I could have, should have, been writing and now my poor novel struggling to be born has been left behind, unrealised, unfinished, aborted, irrelevant, stillborn – OK, this is not what I should be thinking about. So work on PalFest instead. The Palestine Festival of Literature, my other baby that took me away from the novel these five years. Due to happen in under ten weeks and still the money not in place. So, cough and sneeze and write to a potential funder. And cough and sneeze and write to another potential funder—

Omar calls from Tahrir to say that something's different. There are no civilians on the checkpoints and the military are not searching people or bags or looking at IDs any more.

I keep an eye on al-Jazeera as I try to work and suddenly I realise that what I am seeing on the TV screen in the corner of my living room is a camel and horses galloping into Tahrir – yes, indeed: a camel with a colourful tasselled saddle and stirrups – a pyramid camel, in fact, decked out to attract tourists and to pose for photographs, and his bright tassels are tossing about and the horses are prancing and dashing and people are running and circling round them and without taking my eyes off the screen I try to call Omar but I can't get through so I call my sister who has just got in from the airport where she was collecting Alaa, her son (named after my brother), and Manal, his wife, who are coming home from South Africa to join the revolution. She is so happy; I get her typical big laugh that doesn't end when she starts to speak but runs through her words so sometimes you have to ask her to repeat what she's saying – but this time she's so happy and there's so much background noise that she's shouting loud and clear: 'It's OK it's OK,' she shouts and laughs. 'They attacked us with horses and camels but we've captured them and the kids are having rides on them in the Midan and everything's fine and Alaa and Manal are with me.'

My sister is a force of nature; a rebel child who became the backbone of the family; a brilliant mathematician who dedicated her professional life to saving her students: intellectually, morally and physically; a radical Romantic who has spread her sheltering wings over friends and family and

brought up three children who've shone like comets in the
skies of our revolution. Over the years, I've tagged along
with her to protests – outside the central police station
in Garden City, on the steps of the Journalists' Union,
Downtown, at the Courthouse in Alexandria – always
trying to edge nearer to the centre, always cordoned off,
blocked by Central Security that was always at least five
times our number. I once asked whether she wasn't afraid.
And the answer came back simply: no.

Once, on a protest near the university, one of her most
brilliant students, fresh back from Britain with a Ph.D.
earned in record time, was jostled and pushed, his glasses
were knocked off his face and he got down on the ground
to find them and a Central Security soldier, smelling blood,
moved in and she just hurled herself between her felled
student scrabbling for his spectacles on the ground and
the booted kick swinging for his head. 'You animal!' she
yelled at the helmeted, shielded, jackbooted soldier. 'You
animal! Have you any idea what that head is worth?' And
later, laughing over coffee: 'All the years and the effort I
put into that boy and the bastard was going to finish him
off for me in a second!' My sister makes a personal invest-
ment in everything and everyone who crosses her path.

I nurse a fever, take lozenges with cortisone for my
throat, try to write. Egyptian state TV is lying so shamefuly
I cannot watch it. We should have taken Maspero on the
29th, I think for the hundredth time. I follow news on
satellite channels and Twitter. The people who last night
were listening to music in Tahrir and debating modes
of government – my nieces and nephew, my son, their
friends and all the shabab and everyone who has come to

the Midan because they want a better life for their country
– will now be putting their bodies on the line – again. It's
all they have. The Mubarak baltagi militias have sticks and
stones, and swords and chains, and dogs and trucks. And
the military stands by and does nothing. On the news I can
hear thousands of voices raised in the angry chant: 'Wa7ed,
etnein, / el-geish el-Masri fein?' (One, Two / Army, where
are you?) And then again: 'Selmeyya! Selmeyya!'

Alaa, my nephew, went into administrative detention in
2005 for supporting the Egyptian judiciary's move for
independence. The regime kept him for forty-five days.
He was in Tora, the same jail which had held his father,
Ahmad Seif, for five years in the early eighties for Leftist
political activism. My sister could not bear to visit him.
She, so definite and loud and – *there*, she went quiet and
blurred and lost. Our nanny, old, and wrinkled and losing
her sight, berated her in her distress: 'Are you happy now?
Content? You brought him to this. Every day protests,
protests and big talk. Now we've lost the boy because of
you.' And Laila didn't even answer. Until he came out
of jail no one could comfort her. Now, he's back from
his job in South Africa with Manal. The revolution is in
full swing. Ahmad Seif is running the amazing team at
HMLC and they're at the heart of the practical and legal
support for the revolution. Mona is doing her brilliant lab
work and her brilliant communications work. That just
leaves Sanaa, seventeen, who lives in her head but who's
also in the Midan with her friends: taking notes, collecting
information. She still has her school finals to get through.
Later tonight, she and her friends will take refuge from

the fighting in an apartment high up above Tahrir. Over the hours they will transform into the editorial board of *el-Gurnal*: the first independent newspaper to come out of the Midan.

I call Omar and he says the baltagis are attacking and there are battles at three entrances to the Midan and the shabab have formed defence lines. He says that they can see trucks driving up behind the attackers.

There is one useful side to all this: it will nip in the bud any sympathy that started up for Mubarak after the show we were treated to last night. Once again the regime displays its banality; unable to come up with any move that is decent or innovative, it resorts to its usual mix: last night it serves up a sentimental tear-jerker, then it can't even wait for its possible effect but gets right back to obtuse brutality. It is its nature.

Mubarak's baltagi militias attack Tahrir from Qasr el-Nil Bridge in the west, from four streets on the eastern side, and from the main northern entrance that runs alongside the Museum. The shabab's first act is to secure the Midan's entrance from Tahrir Street, to protect the little field hospital in the Mosque of the Servants of the Compassionate. The army makes sure to block off one street, Qasr el-Eini, which leads to the Ministries and the Cabinet Office. Other than that it stands aside.

All day long the baltagis swarm the entrances and the shabab beat them back. Midan Tal3at Harb becomes the baltagi headquarters for the day and the whole of Downtown is the scene of running battles as the baltagis retreat from the entrances, regroup and attack again. For several hours the periphery of the Midan is a fierce battle zone, while in its heart children have rides on the captured horses and the Midan lives the life it's developed over the last four days. The Battle of the Camel; the same tactics that have been used against us, against every protestor over the last five years, the same tactics used at the last elections to scare voters off the streets, have reappeared and with redoubled viciousness. This is the regime that promises to listen to the people and use the coming months to put in reforms.

Their next trick will be to say that the young people in Tahrir are 'foreign' elements, that they have connections to 'terrorism', that they've visited Afghanistan, that they want to destabilise Egypt. But by now the whole world knows what Ali-who-couldn't-speak always knew: that this regime lies as naturally as it breathes.

Omar calls and I can hear the roar of chaos in the background and he says, all bored and laconic: 'Could you talk to this officer who's trying to take me away and tell him I'm Egyptian and I'm your son?'

'Yes,' I say. 'Hello?'

Now I can hear a man saying: 'I'm not going to talk to anyone. I want you to come with me—'

'You said you'd talk to any relative who—'

'I'm not talking to anyone. I suspect you—'

'Hello! Hello!'

'We have been arguing for half an hour and you finally said—'

'I'm an officer in the army and I suspect you—'

'Hello! Talk to me!'

'Talk to my mother.'

'And I suspect you—'

'Talk to ME! TALK TO ME!'

'It's OK. Leave it,' my son says into the phone and the line goes dead. I keep calling him back and getting unavailable.

An hour later I call and get him. The noise in the background is intense. 'What happened?' I shout.

'With what?'

'With the army?'

'It's OK, it's OK. I got rid of him. People helped.'

7.00 p.m.

Channel 4 News' fixer calls and says they can't send a car to take me to the studio because they can't accept responsibility for my safety.

The studio they're using is between the Ramses Hilton and the Radio and Television building, with the entrance in the alleyway running behind the Maspero Corniche. On a normal day it would be a twenty-minute walk from my house.

9.00 p.m.

I know it must seem strange to the garage chaps. I appear out of the darkness and they have to move cars to clear a path for mine to leave. I apologise. The garage entrance

has no gate and so they've blocked it with a massive black
4 x 4. It has to be moved for me to drive out and will have
to be moved again for me to drive back in. I'm putting
them to a lot of trouble. 'Work,' I say, and make a help-
less little flutter with my hands. In other words: I am not
a mad person driving out into the night in the middle of a
blackout and a curfew on a whim.

And so I drive through two neighbourhood checkpoints
– they apologise for the inconvenience they're causing me,
I thank them for the security they're providing – and on
to 15 May Bridge. A man on the approach to the bridge
taps on my window.

'There's trouble Downtown,' he says. 'Don't go.'

'I have to,' I say. 'Work.'

'Well,' he says doubtfully, 'take care.'

From the bridge I glance down at Maspero and see that
the tanks are still in place around the R&T building. I
pass my beloved derelict Khedivial Stables with the horses'
heads which seem even more weird and ghostly tonight.
I'm asking myself if two minutes on the news in the UK
is worth this. But that's not why I'm doing it, really. I'm
doing it because I want to be closer to whatever's happening in Tahrir. And I will not be stopped from moving
around my own city. This is the route I used to walk
with my nanny when I was eight. Before they put up this
flyover. When we used to walk across Abu el-Ela Bridge
to buy fresh chicken, and to buy salted fish for Shamm
el-Neseem. And later with my friends to walk into town,
to the shops and the movies. I miss the old iron bridge
and I hate this flyover but I won't be made into a fright-

ened stranger ten minutes from my home. I descend into
Boulac.

The spookiest thing is the absence of people; how the
streets are deserted. Cairo streets are never empty. There
are always people walking, men sitting outside their shops,
youths loitering, people spilling out of coffee shops and
juice shops, gathered around food stalls. Even in the dead
hours between three and five in the morning there will
be street cleaners and nightwatchmen and men sitting
in the doorways of greengrocers' and bakeries and pharmacies that stay open all night. In winter, often huddled
around a small fire in a brazier. First-time visitors to the
city always think something extraordinary is happening,
a fiesta perhaps, to bring all these people out on to the
streets. Me, I've never been in an empty street except in
London or Washington, DC. Now the emptiness spooks
me. I resist locking my car doors.

There's a barricade at the intersection with Gala2 Street.
The young men guarding it look rougher than the ones
back in Zamalek. Actually, I'm not sure whether they're
Popular Committee or State Security in civvies, or even
baltagis. But I open the window and show my driver's
licence and ID and they wave me through.

Boulac rose against the French in 1798. The French
captured one of the leaders of the revolt, Mustafa
el-Besheiti. They put down the revolt, shelled the neighbourhood and laid Boulac to waste. Then they released
el-Besheiti to the people and the people killed him.

I pass the hospital where I was born and park just before
the Ramses Hilton. There are three other cars. The man
looking after them says it'll be ten pounds now because

it's so dangerous. I don't know if he's the regular guy who parks cars or a baltagi; how can you tell? I'll assume everyone is a good person until I'm proved wrong. Not a hundred metres away, the battle rages. My sister and her children are there. My friends are there. My son is there. I'm sure he's balanced on something high so that he can get a good view for his camera.[28] I shut the image out and phone the fixer and she says she'll come and get me and not to walk alone. I walk anyway and meet her and two young men and they take me into the building down through the garage and up the back stairs because the normal entrance is locked and barricaded. Upstairs it's buzzing: several stations are broadcasting out of the flat, every studio is working and – no big deal – many people have made it here. Tomorrow the baltagis will arrive on the doorsteps of this and every studio in the neighbour-hood and they'll give them a choice: close down or we'll smash all your equipment. But tonight the studios are tell-ing the world what's happening over there in the Midan.

And what's happening is one of the decisive battles of the revolution. The regime's forces have been pushed back from Qasr el-Nil and all the eastern entrances, and now, at 10.00 p.m., are concentrating their attack on this northern approach to Tahrir; the wide road that runs out of Midan Abd el-Menem Riyad and then is flanked on the east by the Franciscan School and some residential buildings, and on the west by the Museum. And crossing over the road is a section of 6 October Flyover. The shabab have captured some baltagis and their IDs showed them to be Central Security soldiers. Anyone they capture they copy their ID then turn him over to the military. Now the shabab have beaten the regime's force back from the road itself but it's taken up position on the flyover – and it has men on the roof of one of the higher apartment blocks by the school. The shabab can see these people. What they can't see are the snipers positioned on the roofs of the Museum and the Hilton. But from time to time they spot a green laser beam shining into their lines. And they suspect that this means snipers.

From the flyover and from the roof the regime hurls its usual missiles at the citizens: stones and shards of ceramic and marble, bottles and Molotov cocktails. Fireballs land in the midst of the crowd below. The shabab gain access to the roof of the next-door building. Stones and Molotovs are exchanged roof to roof, but the regime has the advantage: it has the higher roof. And on the flyover it is using ambulances and Central Security trucks and civilian mini-buses to bring in new cargoes of fighters and ammunition.

The battle is fought across the statue of the shaheed Abd el-Menem Riyad, the Chief-of-Staff of the Egyptian army during the 'War of Attrition' with Israel. Riyad was killed by an Israeli shell, with his men in Trench No. 6 by the Suez Canal on 9 March 1969. 'A leader's place is with his men,' he had said, and now his face is turned towards the citizens defending the Midan.

The citizens have fallen into battle formation. Older people are the supply lines and they tear the corrugated metal fencing from the mysterious building site next to them and the stones from the pavements. Runners pile the stones into blankets and run them to the front. The shabab on the front line pitch the stones and hold up a shielding wall of corrugated iron. They can't see past their shield so they follow the directions of a maestro standing further back, high up on the burned-out shell of an armoured personnel carrier. A few metres behind the front line another line stands. These are the substitutes. When a 'forward' falls, a substitute takes his place. And a few metres behind the substitutes are three lines of the next 'forwards'. At a signal, they will step in to give their friends a rest. In the middle of the lines, groups stand on the tops of upturned vehicles; they keep the flag flying and the information flowing. Rations of water and bread pile up. The first lot of crash helmets to be brought in is given to the young women paramedics and the women doctors and nurses giving emergency treatment behind the lines. Bad cases are rushed across the Midan to the field hospital in the Mosque of the Servants of the Compassionate. Anyone who's not busy drums. A loud, energetic, rhythmic drumming drumming drumming on the metal sheets. This is the sound of the citizens, the voice of the revolution. They keep it up all night long. It tells any approaching regime baltagi that the shabab are awake and waiting and it helps to keep everybody going; it says we're here, we're here, we're undefeated.

On the 25th, the first day of the revolution, when the regime choked Tahrir with gas and attacked the first waves of protestors with truncheons and shotguns, people found refuge in residents' flats nearby. My friend Ghada Shahbandar eventually decided she would leave her refuge and a young man volunteered to accompany her to her car. On the steps he told her he was a butcher and had looked at his knives that morning and considered. 'But then,' he said, 'I reckoned we really wanted to keep it selmeyya so I didn't bring any.' He held her arm to run her to her car and as they ran he was taken. 'I tried to hold him,' she says, 'but they took him. In Tal3at Harb Street. He was on the ground and five men were kicking him. Baltagis.' Every few metres, she said, there would be a group gathered around a fallen young man kicking his head in.

On the 28th the regime was taken by surprise. They had not expected to be so comprehensively beaten in Cairo, in Suez, in Alexandria. Now they've regrouped and they're back. Not with official forces but with their paramilitary thug militias: the baltagis, and some of their soldiers and conscripts in baltagi-type clothing. Later we will discover that one of the organisers of today is the National Democratic Party Member of Parliament for Nazlet el-Semman, the neighbourhood at the foot of the Pyramids where many of the camelmen and horsemen live. He is also the owner of the massive Ceramica Cleopatra, from whose factory floors come the shards that are splitting our heads open.

The army could stop all this in a minute. It doesn't. At one point a sole officer fires his gun into the air.

I finish my broadcast and hesitate. The shivers and aches are worse. But the battle for Tahrir is taking place not a hundred metres from where I'm parked. Somewhere in there my nieces are manning communications with the outside world, my son is filming the battle. But to go in I would have to somehow cross the battle line. I phone one last time: is there anything any of you need? No. What should I do? Go home. Now.

Jon Snow walks me back to my car. How many ways

can this government disgrace itself? Would they destroy the country rather than leave?

On Monday the 7th there will be a TV interview with Tarek Helmy, our top heart surgeon. He will say that he's not a revolutionary but had gone into Tahrir tonight because his son was in the sit-in and he wanted to see it for himself. He got caught in a fight between two groups of young men and stepped forward to talk them down. And, just as he thought he'd made peace, stones came flying from the back lines of one group. He shielded himself with a corrugated iron sheet and watched and he said he had no doubt then who was on the side of right. He said one side fought with courage and the other, where the peace-breaking stones had come from, was both brutal and cowardly. He said he'd phoned his hospital and asked for medical supplies. His son-in-law filled a car with everything you needed for a field hospital and drove it across Qasr el-Nil Bridge and the baltagis stopped him and beat him up. They emptied the car. Till that point, he said, he'd thought, OK, they have their wounded, too. But then, he said, they threw all the medical equipment, all the supplies, into the river. He knew then that he would not leave Tahrir till the revolution had been won.

I drive back. I take my time. The streets are dark but I've gone out and done my thing, and the shabab are holding Tahrir. If we, the pro-democracy movement, win this battle, the spirit that inspires Tahrir will pervade the country. In the Midan, every shade of the political spectrum is represented. The Left is here, and the Liberals. The Muslim Brotherhood, the Gama3at Islameyya and the Salafis are officially not joining, but their shabab

have rebelled and they're with us too, making up an estimated 10 per cent of the people in the Midan. Our society
is rich and complex and varied and we revel in it. The
people here are so way ahead of their government. If you
could see the kids on the street telling you that the regime
wants to pin the responsibility for this movement on the
Islamists in order to scare the West. If you could see the
small field hospitals with their volunteer doctors – mostly
young women – and the medicines pouring in from well-
wishers. If you could see the young men with their jeans
worn low and the tops of their coloured boxers showing form a human chain to protect what the people have
gained over the last week in the streets of our country.
If you could see my nieces hanging banners from balconies . . . you would know beyond a shadow of a doubt:
Egypt deserves its place in the sun – out of the shadow of
this brutal regime.

Thursday 3 February

I've woken up much better and the Internet's working
although it's slow. Our mobiles work but we can't send
messages. The only messages that come through are from
the SCAF, urging us to behave responsibly! Everyone
phones to check up on everyone else. The grocer calls to
ask if we need anything and we ask for bread, milk, tea,
eggs, biscuits, cheese . . .

  Lulie is staying with me. We have breakfast, read

the papers. I slowly answer some emails. Then we get the phone call with the news about Ahmad Seif, Laila's husband, and I send out a last message before we leave the house:

Date: Thu, 3 Feb 2011 13:05:47
A good friend just saw 8 to 12 people being dragged out of No 1 Souq el-Tawfikeyya St and bundled into a civilian microbus while a military police vehicle waited near by. The people were being beaten and the street had been told they were 'Iranian and Hamas agents come to destabilise Egypt' so the street was chanting against them. No 1 Souq el-Tawfikeyya St is the home of the offices of the Hisham Mubarak Legal Centre, the Centre for Social and Economic Rights and the 6th April Youth.

And, btw, my brother-in-law, the lawyer Ahmad Seif, *is* the Legal Centre.

Please get word out to as many news outlets as you can.

I call Ismail in London to make sure he's got the email and will get it out. I call my sister and we arrange to go into the Midan together; to meet by the Andalus Gardens. Then we head out.

As we park we meet relatives and friends. Everyone walking to Tahrir is carrying something: blankets, bottles of water, medical supplies. Lots of us are taking mobile charge cards for the people in the sit-in. As we get to the middle of the bridge three men come towards us and we know straight away they're not friends. We automatically

form into a tight phalanx. They're grabbing at the blankets and the first aid bags and shouting that we have to
be searched, that these things have to be delivered to an
'official station'. We shout louder. In fact we scream as we
beat them off: 'Get away from us! Get away from us!' This
is the first time I've screamed in the street. We're holding on to our supplies and on to each other and we keep
moving. My sister hits the man who's trying to grab her
bag. She has even less patience than usual today because
of Ahmad Seif and his comrades. We have no idea where
they've been taken. My sister says Ahmad had told her that
if this happened we should not spend time looking for him
but should concentrate on holding Tahrir, on making the
revolution work.[29]

The men snatch at our supplies and call us spies and
whores. Activists run forward from the Midan to help us
and we reach the shabab's checkpoint and are thoroughly
and politely searched: men by men, women by women.
Two army soldiers stand by. A young activist asks us to
give the soldiers two blankets; he says the men have been
there for two days with no cover. The soldiers demur but
eventually take the blankets.

In the Midan the mood is sober, determined, indignant. The disinformation, the smears being spread by the
government, are hurting – perhaps more than the wounds
and bruises so many people are carrying. That this regime
should dare to say that the protestors are agents of Israel,
Iran and Hamas – suddenly able to put aside their differ-
ences and work together – beggars belief. This is what
people are talking about. This, and the insult of being
attacked by thugs on camels and horses, and that women

leaving the Midan yesterday were roughed up, insulted and robbed. And that there's no turning back.

I'm supposed to do a TV interview at 6.30. I phone the recording studio at 4 Gala2 Street and they tell me they're closed. 'They came round,' they say, 'with sticks. And threatened to smash everything up if we didn't close.'

I go to look at the front line of yesterday's battle. The pavements are broken up and the corrugated-metal sheets are stacked in case they're needed again. 'Don't assume treachery, but be on your guard': men lie on the treads of the army tanks to prevent them moving. The regime's baltagis have been beaten back but they're regrouping on the flyover. Lines of young men with linked arms protect the entrance to the Midan. The clinic that was set up when the baltagis were beaten back hums with activity. Doctors in white coats change dressings on wounds, take details. Two lawyers – in their legal court gowns – take statements. A woman sees me writing and comes up: 'Write,' she says, 'write that my son is in there with the shabab. That we're fed up with what's been done to our country. Write that this regime divides Muslim from Christian and rich from poor. That it's become a country for the corrupt. That it's brought hunger to our door. Our young men are humili-ated abroad while our country's bountiful. Be our voice abroad. Tell them this is a national epic that will be taught in schools for generations to come. We've been in Tahrir since Friday and the whole Midan was sparkling. Look what they've done to it! But look! Look at that micro-bus: twelve people on it at all times and the banners never came down and the flag never stopped waving. The army stopped the ambulances from coming in but these young doctors – they sewed up the shabab on the pavement. My son, it took an hour to dig out the pellets from his legs. And then he went back in—' Everybody, everybody here has become an orator. We have found our voice.

The regime has rid itself of one of its central pillars: Habib el-Adli, the Minister of the Interior, is under house arrest. A new general takes over the Ministry and we get news that thirty-nine more people have been kidnapped. Among them seven of the young organisers of the revolution – kidnapped from the street after a meeting with Muhammad el-Baradei. A friend phones to say many Egyptian Christians have declared three days of fasting; fasting for victory.

My sister comes up with her friend and colleague Hani al-Hosseini. He has blood running down his face. He says he was detained by the military who refused to believe he was a university professor and beat him up. He says they dragged him into the Egyptian Museum and there are people there tied up and being beaten. We set about forming a delegation; we find two friends, a surgeon and an architect, and our group of five walks up to the tanks by the Museum and requests to speak to the officer in charge. A brigadier comes to talk to us. He's totally wooden and persistently denies that anything is going on in the Museum. We give him an out by suggesting maybe it's going on without his knowledge. He doesn't like this. We say if he goes in and comes back and gives us his word that there's no one in there we'll believe him and go away. He says he will but he doesn't move. Eventually I make a little speech about dignity and iconic buildings and how shameful it is that the Egyptian army should be torturing people inside it. His jaw tightens and he says: 'They're not inside the Museum; they're in the garden.' We go and give statements to the lawyers in the field hospital.

Later we're to find out that the Museum was, in fact, used as a holding station for detainees, and they were mistreated. Rami Essam, who became famous for his guitar-accompanied songs in Tahrir, had burns and stripes on his back from the hours he spent there. He was released but many others went from the Museum to military trials and are now in jail.

Friday 4 February

Morning and I'm leaving for Tahrir. My family is already there. Omar phoned and said it's fine: the checkpoints are back up and everything's orderly.

It's become a tradition: Friday and Tuesday we get at least a million people out on the streets. Last Friday, the 28th, was 'Day of Wrath', today is 'Day of Departure' – Mubarak's, we hope. It's also become a tradition that Friday (Muslim) prayers in Tahrir are followed by (Christian) Mass – with everybody joining in both sets of 'Amens'. This is the first time I am moved by a Friday sermon. Sheikh Mazhar Shaheen, the young imam of Omar Makram Mosque, speaks what's on people's minds and links our actions to spiritual values. He addresses his sermon to 'Egyptians' and he speaks of 'Christ's example'. He ends by praying to God to: 'Make us stand fast. Restore

our rights. We want not war but peace. Bear witness that
we love Egypt and hold the dust of this land dear. Restore
our dignity. Unite us and let not our blood be spilled.'
Our great communal 'Amens' roll through the Midan.

   The questions that are being settled on the streets of
Egypt are of concern to everyone. The paramount one is
this: can a people's revolution that is determinedly democratic, grassroots, inclusive and peaceable succeed?

4.00 p.m.

Delegations from many Egyptian cities and governorates
are here. The regime has stopped the trains running but
people have got here anyway. The flags and banners of
Alexandria, Assiut, Beheira, Herghada, Port Said, Qena,
Sohag, Suez and others are flying. The chant is: 'El-
shar3eyya m'nel-Tahrir.' Legitimacy comes from Tahrir.

8.00 p.m.

The baltagis have stayed in the side streets. The Midan is
well defended, and has provided all day – as in the other
days of peace we've had – a space for debate. Many ideas
for moving forward are being articulated and discussed.
Older people are still hopeful of democracy, longing for

the clean elections, the representative government they've longed for all their lives. Some of the shabab argue that we're beyond – the world is beyond – the old forms of democracy; that for the last twenty years every movement with energy has come from outside the traditional frameworks, that the static structures of the nation-state and the fluid power of capital cannot coexist without leading to repression. What we have in Tahrir is the opposite of a vacuum; we have a bazaar of ideas on the ground. We are full of hope and ideas, and our gallant young people are guarding our periphery.

Saturday 5 February

Rushing around. Word is that people are being snatched from the fringes of the Midan. Two young women activists were taken by baltagis, but they were freed by two army officers and taken to safety in an ambulance. Six activists have disappeared.

I wish I could stay in Tahrir all day. I'm doing so many interviews I seem to be talking all the time. I'm tired of my voice. And I can hardly get it out anyway. Thank goodness there are no traffic rules and no traffic police any more. I just drive the shortest way, park anyhow, run in and speak, then out and start all over again.

I get a transcript of our friend, Maysara's, testimony. He was snatched by baltagis in Tal3at Harb Street but it was the military who beat him up – in the Museum. And he was moved around other locations and beaten up – in an ambulance. He says they weren't all vicious and he says they really think the revolution is being pushed by paid outside forces.

I also get a chronology, a history of our new Vice-President and long-time Head of Intelligence, Omar Suleiman. It details his extensive, personal involvement in rendition and torture. The Midan, of course, knows everything: 'No Mubarak, No Suleiman / No more agents for the amrikan.'

There's no news yet of Ahmad Seif and his colleagues. Or, rather, we know that they're detained by Military Intelligence, but that's all we know. While they were being taken, one of them left his mobile on and a transcript has come out of what was heard. Again, the accusations were all of being spies and traitors: 'If you walk out on the street now the people will kill you: they know what you are.'

I know that if I could go to the Midan for a bit I would feel better and my spirits would rise. But I can't. I finish with the BBC Arabic and race home just ahead of the team that's coming to do an interview for an Indian TV channel.[30] I had suggested I could go to their hotel but they said they'd been threatened and the hotel had been told not to let them film. I'm uncomfortable but I welcome them in and two minutes later my doorbell rings again. It's the concierge's daughter and she wants to know who the two women are who just came up. I stare: 'They're my guests.' 'This is your home,' she says, 'and you must do as you please. But the plainclothes have been round, they're asking who lives in each flat and they're asking about foreigners and about media people, and we have to report to them if foreigners or media people come round. How long are your guests staying?' 'They'll have their visit and leave,' I say. I close the door and I make tea. I call Omar and he says we should sleep at my brother's. When the interview's over I ask the two journalists to wait. I throw a few things into a bag and I leave with them. This flat has been my home, on and off, since I was seven. Now I feel uncomfortable and alien in it.

The garage attendant has to move the 4 x 4 again. I apologise and say I hadn't meant to go out again; family emergency: I won't come back tonight. But then it's time for the *Democracy Now!* interview and I no longer feel comfortable giving the interview while I drive; I feel I need to be alert to the street. I sit in the dark garage and talk to America for an hour.

Tuesday 8 February

There's a small, cracked, black-and-white photograph that shows my father's family deployed on one of the narrow terraced lawns of the Andalus Gardens. Something keeps bringing me back to this picture: my grandmother, in a demure dark coat, sits with her legs tucked under her, her two daughters one on either side of her. My small father, his hands in the pockets of his short trousers, stands a little apart, in that borderline aloof, slightly arrogant positioning that he is to maintain throughout his life. They were on that step over there, just across from where I'm sharing a sunny bench with Omar.

We're only here briefly, my son and I; a fleeting moment, captured when I said, as he walked me from my car to Tahrir. 'Could we go in here for a moment? I don't think I've been since I was ten'. 'Sure', he said glancing quickly at his mobile. We clasp our glasses of hot tea and share – though we shouldn't – a cigarette. A limestone Ahmad Shawqi, Prince of Poets, sits pensively to our right. The Nile runs behind us and the sun shines upon us and we speak of concerts and screenings that could happen in this space. Because everything is possible now; such is our confidence – it's just a matter of time. Hours – perhaps.

For the last twenty years my main feeling as I pass the Andalus Gardens has been dread; dread that one of the regime's intimates would be able to commandeer it and 'develop' it as they've done with so much else in the country. I would search for telltale signs of impending brashness and be relieved to see the dusty old municipal noticeboard still in place. Today the dread has evaporated; suddenly I'm thinking what a great place this will be for music in our new, recovered city.

Omar is answering phone calls. If I get up from this bench and run down the nine steps that dip through this charming amphitheatre, and through the narrow fountained rectangle at the bottom, and up another – maybe six – steps on the other side I'll be right there where my grandmother sits, where my father stands. A cracked black-and-white photo. Since I was a child I've been intrigued by it: there's the garden, so distinctive, familiar, unchanged, except that there also is my father, as small as

me, a million years ago. Other pictures exist of my father
in Boy Scout uniform in the desert, or with his family
posed against the Pyramids or against a river backdrop.
But these things were given, permanent parts of life; you
knew you shared them with the whole world since the
beginning of history. Is that it, then; that this small, urban,
constructed, specific part of my neighbourhood should be
so unchanged when change has so marked the four people
photographed against it? My grandmother, Neina, old and
strict ever since I knew her and yet – here's a memory: I'm
loitering behind her in the kitchen of the Abdeen flat while
she whips up a treat for me at the cooker: 'sadd el-hanak',
the 'mouth-stopper'; flour and brown sugar fried quickly
in butter and arranged in spoon-shaped petals on a china
plate. I eat it on the small balcony where, angled sideways,
I can see the palace that's also pictured in the schoolbook
on the table in front of me. There are the iron railings, and
behind them the low far-flung building, and in between
the railings and the palace, the courtyard – empty now but
in my book it's teeming with people: on the left stands the
Khedive Tewfik, flanked by Sir Charles Cookson and Sir
Auckland Colvin, on the right and facing him a melee of
troops of the Egyptian army, on horseback and on foot. At
their head stands Ahmad Orabi Bey in military uniform,
in the act of sheathing his sword. The caption reads: 'We
are slaves to no one and will be inherited no longer.' 1881.
That's 120 years ago – and we're saying it again today.

Earlier

I woke up to voices sounding as though they were with me in the room:

'The army'll stage a coup—'

'They don't need to. They'll wait and take it peeled and ready—'

'Suleiman is army – isn't Suleiman army?'

'Enough military; we've had a bellyful of military—'

'A parliamentary republic—'

'No, no: Egypt has to have a president – a leader—'

In Zamalek I'm on the sixth floor. Here, at my brother's, I'm on the second. In Wimbledon I sleep on the ground floor but there's never anyone talking outside. Except if they're drunk in the middle of the night and the police come.

Bright sunlight. I get out of bed and look out of the window: cigarette smoke rising, keys jingling, a group of men by the front door. I can't get over these open discussions of politics you hear everywhere now; not just in the Midan but every-where the conversations you overhear are political: systems of government, education, public versus private ownership . . . what weight of repression was keeping all this down?

I glance into Mariam's room: a whirlwind of shoes, hair-brushes, tops, necklaces, on the floor, the bed, the chairs; ribbons hanging from mirrors, silver cups on bookcases, hundreds – well, tens – of medals, cups, trophies. Salma's is just the same, with a few extra Egyptian flags: you don't know whether you're backstage in a theatre or in a club locker room.

★   ★   ★

I like being at my brother's. Apart from having to stop by Zamalek to pick up clothes or papers – or hairbrushes or necklaces – I like being here; back in the heart of a noisy, argumentative, varied family with lots of friends in and out.

The living room has last night's tea glasses, chocolate wrappers and orange peel. The cushions are still squashed and scattered from where we sat: my brother in his armchair, Sohair next to him in her upright with the back support, Omar – having inherited from Khalu the ability to simultaneously sleep and participate – stretched out full length on a commandeered sofa, the girls on floor cushions, me perched on the arm of a chair, near the exit, always only there for a minute and about to go and work.

Ahmad Seif and his colleagues from the Legal Centre had been released unharmed, the shabab of the Popular Committee were on the barricades outside, my sister and Mona, Alaa and Sana were in Tahrir, and we watched heart surgeon Tarek Helmy's testimony about Wednesday's battle reel in anybody who hadn't already been captured by Wael Ghonim.

Ghonim had come straight to the '10 p.m.' Dream TV studio from eleven days in detention; eleven days blindfolded and under interrogation. He looked haggard and he was twitchy with tension. They'd snatched him from Tahrir on the 28th.[31] He spoke of how for eleven days his parents and wife hadn't known where he was. He cried and collected himself and spoke again. He hadn't wanted it known that he was the admin for the Khalid Said Facebook page which had got people into the streets on the 25th. But he'd been outed now and he had something

to say. He started with the shuhada: 'I want to say to all
parents whose children have died – they are shuhada with
God. I want to say we never thought we'd – even break
anything, let alone kill a person.' And when the anchor
showed the pictures of Ahmad Bassiouny, Islam and
the other young men, he ended, in tears, with the shuhada:
'To every mother and every father whose child has died: I
swear it's not our doing. It's the doing of the people who
held on to power and wouldn't let go.'[32] Overcome, and
weeping, he stumbled off the set. But he'd done enough;
he'd spoken with passion about the allegiance of the shabab
to Egypt: 'We are not traitors – we love Egypt. Don't
treat us like We're being pushed by someone.' He'd stated
again the big aims of the revolution: to restore dignity
and a sense of belonging to every person, to end corruption and to run Egypt for the benefit of its citizens. He'd
begged us to 'put aside the past for a while and think what
we'll look like in the future'. And he'd restated what we
all knew we needed: a new security apparatus and a new
Constitution, a transitional government formed by the
Head of the Constitutional Court moving towards free
and fair elections. He sounded like every young protestor on the streets of Egypt; this was an authentic voice of
the revolution arriving on the TV screen, and we knew it
would carry to those who had started to lose heart and to
those who, until now, had been unsure.

The day before, Sunday the 6th, the regime had sent
out messages: state radio and TV pumped lies into the
ether: drugs and 'bad things' were happening in Tahrir,
the economy was collapsing, the country was witnessing
a total breakdown of law and order, the President had

promised to consider all legitimate demands, and now the good shabab of Egypt were being led astray by infiltrators from Hamas, from Iran, from Israel, from America – and they were leading the country to its destruction. The new Minister of the Interior inspected the Central Security Forces barracks on TV and talked of redeploying them. State-run organisations resumed work and banks opened. The message was, OK we got the message: now, everything back to normal.

So there's a call for another millioneyya today. I'll go to Tahrir for one o'clock. Meanwhile, I'm producing copy and doing phone interviews at Sohair's dining-room table. Everybody's gone to work and Omar's gone to Tahrir and Um Nagla has arrived and she's clearing up around me, practically dusting my key-boarding fingers, so I stop typing and she tells me how people are worried because there's no police on the streets so I remind her what the police on the streets used to do to people and she agrees but she would still like police on the streets – good police. Well, that's one of the things this revolution is about: good police. And a fair chance for everybody. And healthcare, she says: her husband was as tall as the door and worked all his life and when he fell ill there was nothing. Except for good people who helped her – 'yes, indeed'. I'm on my soap box: 'Your husband. No healthcare, no cover. And how come you don't get a pension for all the years he worked? So God's given you health and you're able to go out to work – what about people who can't work? What should they do? And your daughter, didn't she work in a textile factory? Six days a week, twelve hours a day for thirty-five pounds a week? Tell me what you can buy for thirty-five pounds. And your son: he's working at a gas station. What do they pay him? Nothing. That's right. They give him access to drivers who'll maybe give him tips. You've tried to educate all your kids. Did they get an education? Is Ali staying on at school? No. Why? So what is a government for? Is it there to steal the bounty of this country, the sweat of its labour—'

   'God will punish them,' she assures me, 'God is with you. Ali says the income of the Suez Canal alone would pay off all our debts. Yalla, I'll let you work.' She escapes into the peace of the kitchen and I hear the radio start up: 'and I never knew ... before today-ay ... that eyes could betray ... in this way ... and I never knew ...'

Today will be critical. Yesterday Tora Cement and Suez Textiles came out on strike. We're hoping the 'back-to-normal' strategy will backfire and that once people get back together in the workplace they'll decide to join the revolution. My sister says the academics are going to march. And there will be others.

Early Afternoon

The entrances to the Midan have been narrowed down even more. Sunday night the army tried to move its tanks a few metres into the Midan and fired into the air when people stopped it, and there's a rumour that last night, too, they tried to move. Now they're completely surrounded. People have spread mats and newspapers on the treads and are lying on and around them.

But once you're inside, the Midan is amazing. Even the light in here is different, the feel of the air. It's a cleaner world. Everything's sharper, you can see the leaves on the trees. Badly lopped, they're trying to grow out. Everyone is suddenly, miraculously, completely themselves. Everyone understands. We're all very gentle with each other. As though we're convalescing, dragged back from death's very door. Our selves are in our hands, precious, newly recovered, perhaps fragile; we know we must be careful of our own and of each other's.

The Midan is sparkling clean. The rubbish is piled neatly on the periphery with notices on it saying 'NDP Headquarters'. The fence of corrugated iron stands again around the mystery building site and screens newly constructed washrooms. Lamp posts have put out wires so that laptops and mobiles can be charged. The field hospitals provide free medical care and advice for everyone. A placard reading 'Barber of the Revolution' guides you to a free shave and a haircut. A giant transparent wall of plastic pockets has gone up. The shabab sit next to it. People tell them jokes and they draw or write them and slot them into the pockets; a rising tide of jokes and cartoons. A Punch and Judy show is surrounded by laughing families. A man eats fire. There's face-painting and music and street theatre and a poetry stand.

On Sunday at Christian Mass and Muslim prayers we all prayed together for the young people the regime has been killing since 25 January – and before. Then, in the evening,

there was Omar Suleiman: we watched the veteran intelligence boss interviewed by Christiane Amanpour. Earlier
in the day he had met with sections of the older 'political leadership'– including the Muslim Brotherhood. But
he assured Amanpour that we, the people, don't yet have
'the culture of democracy', that the 'Islamic current' was
pushing us, that the 'other people who have their own
agenda' were pushing us, that the Net and social media
had 'facilitated' our young people 'to talk all together but
is not their idea [sic]; it comes from abroad'.[33] Again he'd
confirmed: in the eyes of the regime we simply could not
be self-propelled. The most we could be was a handcart,
and anybody could throw their rubbish into us and trun-
dle us along. The country fell on its back and kicked its
legs in the air with laughter as he intoned, yet again, for
his American audience that el-Baradei 'has links' with the
'Brother Muslimhoooood' and that 'the Brother Muslim-
hooooood' – are pushing us. Why, we asked, does he speak
in English at all? Why don't these people respect themselves even if they don't respect us? We watched the old
torturer, stiff with formality and self-belief, clinging on to
his simple conspiratorial concepts, holding himself rigid
against the tide, the tsunami of us in the Midan and in the
streets, his thumbscrews and cattle prods for the moment
useless. When he says his message to us is: 'Go home. We
want to have a normal life,' the streets answer with one
voice: 'Mesh hanemshi / Enta temshi!' We're not going /
You go home!

And then, in the Midan, there was a wedding, and then
more music and everywhere there are circles of people
sitting on the ground talking, discussing; ideas flowing

from one group to the other until the most popular find their way to one of the four microphones on the stages. I pause by one group and they immediately invite me to sit. People introduce themselves before they speak. Three civil servants, a teacher, a house painter, two women who work in retail. They talk about what brought them to Tahrir. In the end, the house painter says, it comes down to one thing: a person needs freedom.

There's word that a cold is spreading; people have been sleeping out for twelve days. Everyone coming in brings Vitamin C. A travel agent has emptied his office so that it can be used as a clinic. A call's gone out for tarpaulins. People go to check on the Dakhleyya: the tanks that rescued it from the shabab are still protecting it. The police have locked themselves in and are to be seen crowded behind their windows staring out into the street.

Tahrir is teeming and there are still people flooding in. There's an excited buzz as news comes that a march of 10,000 workers is on its way. Laila phones: there's about 5,000 academics coming along Qasr el-Eini Street; the army has taken down the military barricades at the entrance to Parliament Street and made them go through it and enter Tahrir from Muhammad Mahmoud Street. I walk across to meet them. I've bought fresh mint from a child in the street and brought it and biscuits into the Midan. The courtliness with which people accept the offer of a biscuit! The dignity with which the hungry try to decline! The bow! The hand on the chest! We're all princes here, our manners are impeccable. I walk through the crowd holding a spray of fresh mint in my hand and nobody thinks it strange; they smile and help themselves to a sprig and hold

it to their noses. People move between the different stages
and the different speakers, and people pose by the tanks,
and people kiss the soldiers. By the time I get across the
Midan to meet them my sister and aunt are sitting on the
kerb at the American University corner. A Salafi family
sits next to us and we exchange cakes. My sister says she's
going back to check on Parliament Street because 'we've
left a couple of thousand people to take it over'.

Lulie and I sit side by side on the kerb facing the
Mugamma3 building. Lulie had a small medical 'event' a
few years ago and there's a slight drag to her left leg. She
is, like all the women in my family, gallant and raring to
go – except her body's starting to block her. My mother,
to stop the war on Iraq, marched from Charing Cross to
Hyde Park in and out of her wheelchair, and I saw the
pain in Toufi's knees bring tears to her eyes as she insisted
on climbing yet another set of crumbly stairs to visit yet
another woman in the Productive Families project. Lulie
and I give our bodies a short break on the uneven kerb
and we're both thinking about Toufi because for us the
Mugamma3 building, there, across the road, is Toufi.

That massive curve, like the beginning of an embrace;
you step into it and into a different, darker universe: a
huge lobby funnels upwards into a massive galleried tunnel
soaring up eleven floors and swirling with solid noise, its
air heavy with thousands upon thousands of forms and
applications and stories and desks and chairs and paperclips
and complaints and carbon paper and filing cabinets and
cupboards, crowds of people are in a permanent stampede
crossing and recrossing the giant lobby trying to find the
right staircase the right corridor the right lift and me with

my hand in Toufi's waiting in line for the narrow lift that will, amazingly, carry eight people plus me uncounted up to the seventh floor and her office. All the government departments which deal with actual people are in this building and Toufi works in Social Affairs but she doesn't really do her work in the office but out in the city.

Sitting on the kerb, outside the building, I can feel the noise and bustle and jokes and ribbing of the crowded offices, people squeezing past each other to get to their desks, files files files everywhere, the hunt for someone's missing chair stolen by another office, the maps of the city on the walls as everyone in Outreach sets their routes for the day and yells at the 'buffet' for their coffee and assembles their cases and finishes their paperwork. We'd always stop by the department boss; tall, gentle, greying Uncle Rashad, whose face I can, oddly, see very clearly as I write these words. He had a smile that only crinkled the lines around his mouth a little bit but filled his eyes. And his eyes and eyebrows were very black, like my grandfather's. He stooped, but maybe that was because I was so small. And everybody would disperse into the streets of Cairo: Tante Zeinab, plump and fair and red-haired and loud and always in the highest of slingbacks, Tante Kawthar, dark but green-eyed and a little sad. And Toufi, with that swing to her cropped hair and her full skirt and me holding on to her hand. They dispersed into the streets to make good things happen. We walked through alleys too narrow for cars and we came to the 'sa7at sha3beyya' – the People's Spaces – and wherever we went the kids and the staff were busy around her and Toufi watched the boys play football and looked into the Arts and Crafts Room and admired

the woodwork or sat down to give a quick demonstration of hemming or a neat blanket stitch. She looked at
papers in the admin office and sometimes there was a small
musical performance or a play. The high point of the year
was the Sa7at Sha3beyya Exhibition where the great Cairo
stadium filled with the kids and their families. President
Nasser attended these and I remember one show ending
with a young girl draped in the flag of Egypt holding up
a torch while everyone sang around her. This must have
been before February '58 because the flag was the green
one with the crescent and stars.

My sister says that Nasser is all the proof anyone needs
that the 'Benign Dictator' scenario can never work; no
one could have been cleaner than him, or more on the
side of the disadvantaged – but he set in motion the practices, the systems that led, finally, to Mubarak's regime.
Omar says isn't 'a girl draped in the flag of Egypt . . . etc'
a typical fascist image? I say surely it's fascist only if you're
powerful? We'd just got rid of the King in '52, the British in '54 – and then been attacked by Britain, France and
Israel in '56. Can't we be allowed a girl in a flag?

Time passes and I am in those narrow streets again,
Toufi heavier now, her hair gathered under a grey bonnet,
holding on to my arm over the extra bumpy bits or the
bits where we have to balance on narrow ridges between
stagnant puddles. We go through entrances and up stairs
where we can't avoid brushing the walls with our shoulders even though we walk in single file, and we sit in tiny
rooms taken over by the fabrics and the sewing machines
that Toufi has, in part, come to see have not been sold
or pawned, and Toufi knows the names of all the small

children who come and lean against her and knows which fathers, husbands are in work, out of work, invalided, dead. She listens to the women and looks at their hems and buttonholes and seams and makes sure the leaders of the Productive Families project are delivering linen and thread and collecting finished work and paying cash and sees which women are ready to move on from sewing to cutting and who wants to do a refresher course at the local centre – which is where we go next to check on the preparations for the Productive Families Bazaar: the current high point of the year. The bazaar is held nation-wide but the main one is in Cairo and inaugurated by Mrs Mubarak and by the time the ceremony's over the best pieces have all been reserved by Mrs Mubarak's train of ladies in power to be collected by their drivers next day and never paid for. One year Toufi quietly sold off the best pieces ahead of the bazaar – some pieces went to foreign friends who willingly paid three times the asking price and the money went to the women in the narrow rooms. And word came that if the Project could not produce its usual level of work it would be closed down. So the Productive Families limped along with its well-wishers buying the indifferent stock and the old-style leaders, Toufi, Tante Zeinab etc raising and donating money to keep it afloat.

'Khalas,' I say to Lulie, 'no one's going to rob the Productive Families any more.'

'My sister, habibti,' she says, 'this city used up layers of her. Her legs, her soul.'

We observe the Midan, heaving with bodies, with chants, with flags, with freedom. But where I could see my mother wide-eyed with wonder and delight, I

could only see Toufi cautious, sceptical, a little grim to
be honest. A kind of: this is all very well but where's it
leading? 'Come on, Toufi, it will lead to clean, honest,
transparent government . . . why not? We'll have clean
elections. A government that's accountable to the people,
to Parliament . . .' I hear her typical phrase: 'Let's hope so.'

Later

Tahrir has spread into Parliament Street. The Qasr el–Eini
entrance to the street is a swarm of red berets as the Military Police, wrong-footed, move to block it again. People
are streaming in from the bottom end of the street –
reinforcements for the 2,000 academics. A group of men
get as far as the soldiers and sit down at their feet. One
man, large, fiftyish, eases himself on to the tarmac, glances
up at the soldiers and comments good-humouredly: 'Here
we are. Maybe I've sat down on my grave.'

Blankets and carrier bags of bread and dates and water are
already being stacked by the Parliament walls. We watch the
figures moving behind the windows of the Cabinet Office
and the Ministry of Health. Two shabab start spraying graffiti on the wall of the Cabinet Office. A cleaner comes out
and tells them he's going to have to stay up all night cleaning it. They apologise and put away the spray cans.

Lulie and I sit on the low wall and lean against the railings. Seventeen days from now, on 26 February, at this
same spot, Laila and Mona will see Military Police drag-

ging away a badly beaten young man. My sister will rescue
the young man from the soldiers and put him in a car that
will take him home. Mona wants to keep him till they
can take him home themselves but she's overruled; he's so
unwell he's better off going now. Ten minutes later he's
taken from the car, and this time it's not possible to save
him. Amr el-Beheiri will be tried for 'possessing arms' and
sentenced to five years in el-Wadi el-Gedeed prison in the
Western Desert.

But today we sit and watch the street fill up. We hear
the cheers of the Midan as the Workers' march arrives,
and they bring news that Lafarge Suez and Cairo Tele-
com have come out. And now all the diffused noises and
shouts and bangs and cries of the street get sucked and
unified into one song: the drumming clapping chanting
of the Ultras. The White Knights of the Zamalek Football Club and the Ahlawi of the Ahli Football Club; the
guys who were at the front of the marches on the 25th of
January and broke the police and Central Security lines.
It's always a party when they get to the Midan and now
they're here to seal the takeover of Parliament Street.
They drum and swing and chant their way up the road
just in time to surround the black limo driving out of
the gates of the Cabinet Office. Nobody tries to stop it,
but we drum it on its way. And now people sit and talk
and some of the shabab want to occupy the Parliament
Building, Magles el-Sha3b: 'This the People's Council and we are the People,' but the dominant opinion is
against breaking into anything. They discuss marching on
Maspero since we're all now aware of the harm that state
radio and television is doing us – but again the dominant

opinion is not to break into the building and not to push a confrontation with the army.

I look back now at the spectacle of us, us the people, in all our variety, picnicking, strolling, camping, chanting, on the street of the Ministries between our Parliament and our Cabinet Office; my aunt and I and a few thousand people outside the railings. It would be dead simple to go in and occupy them both. And it's not fear that holds us back. How can these shabab be afraid after their attempt on the Dakhleyya down the road – when for three days they surged against that Fortress of Evil facing bullets and gas? Or after Bloody Wednesday, when they defended the Midan against cavalry and Molotovs and snipers and militias? No, we the people were implementing a doctrine of minimum force, minimum destruction. This was a revolution that respected the law, that had at its heart the desire to reclaim the institutions of state, not to destroy them. It was very clear who its enemy was: the Dakhleyya and State Security and the National Democratic Party. Theirs were the buildings the revolution torched. Even the common soldiers of Central Security were spared – because they were conscripts.

Would we have ended up in a better place if we had been more violent?

When we leave the Midan we walk through two lines of shabab clapping and drumming and encouraging us to sing along: 'We'll come tomorrow / And bring our neighbours / We'll come tomorrow / And bring our friends.'

On Qasr el-Nil Bridge there are stalls selling grilled sweetcorn, cold drinks, peanuts. Soon there will be candy-floss and rice pudding.

Driving home I find the barricades manned by army soldiers alongside the shabab of the Popular Committees. But the soldiers are wearing the armbands of the Committees.

Friday 11 February
Noon

Osta Ashraf is waiting, as arranged, next to the mosque just after the Pyramid underpass. He'd gently reminded me that life doesn't stop just because there's a revolution: 'May God strengthen you all. Our country could be so good if the people running it feared God,' then 'And are you not thinking of coming out to see the land for an hour or so?' The Land! The Land is the little orchard–cum–palm grove near the Pyramids that my mother bought maybe twenty years ago. It's only about half an acre but, with this being Egypt, Kemet, the Land of the Black Earth, it produces in abundance dates and mangoes, limes and melons and whatever vegetables are in season. My mother bought it from Hagg Kamal, a retired schoolmaster, and he continued to look after it for her. She came out every Friday afternoon and they would sit on the stone verandah and talk Leftist politics and he would tell her jokes. When my mother died, at eighty, Hagg Kamal, who was eighty-five, had a stroke. To receive his condolences for my mother I visited him at home and six months later Ala, Laila and I were all there again to offer condolences in turn to his widow and family.

So, now, my mother's children have to look after the
Land, and now the little house on the Land needs fixing
and Osta Ashraf is fixing it for us and that's why he and
I are driving along Pyramid Avenue on this Friday noon
after prayers. I know I'm getting old because as we drive
I'm wondering, yet again, at the changes; at how this urban
sprawl has taken hold in the short space of my adulthood.
I take care not to gaze out of the window and say: 'Imagine . . .' But it really did used to be green fields on either
side; the fields that fed Cairo.

'He's not gone,' Osta Ashraf says.

'No.'

'People were devastated last night.'

'Yes.'

'What's he waiting for?'

Which was indeed the question everyone was asking.

We had been so sure. Wednesday had brought a rolling
wave of strikes: in Kafr el-Sheikh in the Delta thousands
had besieged the Governor's Office, the workers of Petro-
Trade and the Co-op and three other oil companies came
out against Sameh Fahmi, the Minister for Petroleum and
Mineral Resources, the Water and Sewage Workers of
Cairo came out and the Garbage Collectors. The boss of
the National Union of Journalists – a regime man – was
thrown out of his office and the younger journalists of
the government mouthpiece, *al-Ahram*, issued the supple-
ment: *el-Tahrir* in support of the revolution. Everywhere,
people had scented freedom.

Spokespeople and committees had for days been going
off to meet with SCAF to propose Presidential Coun-

cils and Interim Cabinets, and on Thursday SCAF had declared it was in a state of 'permanent convention' to monitor developments and plan how to 'safeguard the nation, its achievements and its ambitions'. The camera, lingering over the generals in their wood-panelled meeting room with the flags and the flowers, seemed to be underlining the absence, for the first time, of the Supreme Commander of the Armed Forces: Hosni Mubarak.

From the afternoon on Thursday everybody was heading for the Midan. We were certain: today would be it. Time passed and passed. The clock on the Arab League building said 8.30. The Midan, all geared up to celebrate, held its breath.

I'm in front of the 'Artists for the Revolution' stage. Like the hundreds of thousands around me, I'm bouncing, waving. West el-Balad (Downtown) are pounding the floorboards. There's no room to dance because we're squashed so close together but everyone's bobbing and swaying and singing along. The uplifted hand of Omar Makram's statue blesses us all and so does the half-moon, further up, nestling – truly – in the fronds of a palm tree. Tahrir is bubbling, bobbing – and so's the whole country. Maybe the whole world. We're waiting. I know my family's in the Midan – but so are a million people. I know we'll all find each other eventually.

Nine thirty and nothing's happened.

Tomorrow we shall learn that while we, the people, were waiting in Tahrir, our soon-to-be-deposed President was on the phone to his friend, the former Defence Minister of Israel, Benjamin Ben-Eliezer. For twenty minutes he complained that America was abandoning him and prophesied that 'civil unrest' would not stop in Egypt but would spread to the whole Middle East and the Gulf.[34]

A hand on my shoulder and it's my brother. I've no idea how he's found me but I hang on to his arm and we work our way through the crowd and we find Sohair and she and I sit on the kerb facing Omar Makram. Some-one brings us tea and we clutch at the glasses, cup them, expose as much as we can of our palms to their warmth. Ala is standing with a group of friends who're discussing whether we're actually in the middle of a military coup and the revolution is about to be turned into a side show. We need a figure, or a group, to step forward and claim the revolution, in Tahrir and with Tahrir behind them. The one individual who could conceivably do this is el-Bara-dei but when he came to Tahrir he couldn't take it and had to leave after fifteen minutes. He doesn't like crowds. Alaa, my nephew, and many of the young people have for days been trying to put together coalitions, governments. Sometimes they've consulted us and we've sat in the street forming Cabinets. But we're in a catch–22 situation: there is no mechanism for Tahrir to select and mandate a group to talk to SCAF. So separate 'leaderships' are taking it upon themselves to do it. And the talks are private; which means that anyone who talks to SCAF now automatically loses credibility with the Midan.

We wait on the kerb. We walk. We join an arguing group. Three young women come and ask if I'm me; they've seen me on television and think I'm 'clean'. One is a doctor, Hoda Yousri, the other two are in the final year of school and want to be journalists. They live in Ma'adi and they've been collecting files on the people who were

killed there on the 28th. They want a good contact in
the media. Hoda also wants a contact who will help her
help the injured. They say more than twenty people have
been killed in Ma'adi and that the police were particularly vicious and let criminals loose on to the people and
started using live ammunition straight off. They say there
was a sniper stationed near the house used by the Israeli
Ambassador and he killed anyone who came within range.
The young women have been collecting information from
families of the dead and injured. They say the area around
Gumhureyya Street is full of posters of shuhada as though
you were in Nablus or Bint Jbeil. We exchange phone
numbers as cries rise from everywhere to 'Hush! Hush!'

Hush.

And, unbelievably, he does not go. And, unbelievably,
he has not understood. And, quite believably, he cannot
change his game. In our millions across the country we
listen to him patronise the shabab: 'speaking to you as a
father', assuring them that the blood of 'your martyrs', the
young people his police and his thugs had killed – more
than three hundred we think – had not been shed in vain,
promising us that he'll move forward and fulfil legitimate
demands – people start angry chants but the Midan shushes
them; we listen intently. He trots out the tired old 'I will
not be dictated to from abroad' trope and we stare at each
other in disbelief; this person who's been doing America
and Israel's bidding for thirty years will not be dictated to
from abroad! When he declares his determination to carry
on 'serving' his country we erupt: 'Don't you understand?
Irhal means depart!' He promises dialogue, waffle, constitutional changes, waffle, he talks about team spirit and

safeguarding the economy and the crowd yells: 'Thief!'
When, twelve minutes in, he starts on the 'I was once
young like you' riff, a great collective groan goes up, and
when he ends with delegating presidential powers to the
Vice-President we erupt.

The Midan is furious and in tears. What will it take?
I write: 'By choosing this path, Mubarak is deliberately
pushing Egypt further into crisis. He is putting the army
in a position where they will soon have to confront either
the Egyptian people or the President and his Presidential
Guard. He is also ensuring that by the time the revolution
is victorious, the military will be in a far stronger position
than when all this started. We are on the streets. There is
no turning back.' People are on the move. Crowds move
to Maspero but still they besiege the Radio and Television
building rather than breaking into it. And others start the
long trek to Urouba Palace, Mubarak's Cairo home.

'He still doesn't understand,' I say to Osta Ashraf.

'He understands,' he says, 'he's just obstinate.'

I call Laila for news. She says that people, millions of
people, people who've never come out before, are moving
into the midans of all the cities, that Tahrir is full.

'This regime would rather see the country ruined than
let go,' Osta Ashraf says. He gets out of the car to open the
gates of the Land.

When I'm here I leave the world behind. For a while.
Except I keep thinking about my mother. Wishing I
hadn't so often wriggled out of coming here when she
asked me. What had I done with those few saved hours
anyway? Wishing I'd done this refurbishment while she

was alive. But she would not have let me. She was opposed to spending money 'unnecessarily'. But maybe she would. And she always liked what I did when I'd done it. Oddly, very oddly, I'd refurbished our madfan, our burial house, just months before she went. I'd wanted to do it for ages but I'd been afraid it would be a bad omen – as though I was expecting it to receive someone. And then, when my father was in hospital for a while, I had his whole flat decorated and all the furniture reupholstered and restored for when he came home and I thought that was so life-affirming that I could afford to slip in the madfan. We gave it a ceiling of pharaonic blue with a band of gold between it and the cream walls. We polished all the stone and brick and marble and bought new plants and put fresh netting on the windows. And five months later my mother was buried there.

Osta Ashraf is holding the gate. He's always so neat and clipped and pressed he could have stepped out of a fifties schoolbook. He wants me to decide how to align the floor tiles. The house is crooked and whatever we do they'll look slightly off anyway. What I'd like to do is align them to the centre and have them be off at the various walls. But the tiler says that can't be done, so I choose, haphazardly, a wall in the kitchen and say we'll align to that.

I go up the ladder to the roof and sit. The Pyramids are there, just beyond those trees. We used to come out to the Pyramids at least once a month. We'd run around in the desert, measure our height against the huge rocks of the lowest rung of the great Pyramid of Khufu, attempt a bit of climbing and have tea in the 'King's Lodge'. (The King, Farouk, had 'Lodges' at the Pyramids, Helwan, Fayyoum, all the beauty spots of Egypt and the 1952 revolution turned them all into cafés for the people.) And always, always, we would stand at the edge of the plateau, looking down towards Cairo, and marvelling at the definiteness of the line between the desert and the green valley; the line this little bit of an orchard is on; the line I'm standing on now.

I need to go to our madfan. I've not visited for a while. My mother, Toufi, Khalu, my grandfather and grandmother – all there. When Omar made his first film, *Maydoum*, he shot a scene in the madfan. They hung up white sheets to reflect the light and weighed them down on the roof with bricks. And a brick came loose and crashed on to his head. For ever now, in bright sunlight, superimposed on the marble sarcophagus of those whom I love but see no longer, I see my son, slowly crumpling to his knees, on his face a look – not of fear or of pain but of intense and interested surprise.

I climb down and discuss the roofing. We'll roof the house with dried palm branches.

Hamed, who looks after the Land, makes me walk to the crumbling end wall. The children climb over it and steal the fruit. He wants me to rebuild it. I haven't the heart to tell him that the fruit he sends us is so plentiful that, even after it's distributed among the whole family, sometimes a few pieces will rot at the bottom of the fridge. I don't mind the children stealing it. I can't tell him that, though, so I say let's not do the wall just yet; enough expense doing the house.

We walk through the Land and pick juicy limes off a tree. Hamed shows me a palm that's collapsed. Why? Its time had come. 'Look at the grace of God,' Osta Ashraf says, 'a palm tree, even when it rots and falls, will fall into a clear space so it hits nothing.' Hamed agrees: 'A palm tree will never cause harm.'

4.00 p.m.

''Bye!'

''Bye!'

''Bye!'

The afternoon is a series of ''byes' and doors slamming as Sohair, my brother, Salma, Mariam and the assorted friends and family who'd been in the house go off to Tahrir. I sit at Sohair's dining table and work on the copy that I'm to complete and file the minute Mubarak has spoken. Would he leave?

I am ready to go the minute I've filed. We've all perfected routines; routines born of five years' experience with baltagis and Central Security. Mine is cotton trousers with zipped pockets over leggings. Actually, the 'cotton trousers' are the pants Egyptian farmers and labourers wear under their galabeyyas. They're wide and loose but with fitted cuffs. They have zipped pockets and draw-string waists and they come in all sizes in beige, grey, navy and white and sell for twenty-five Egyptian pounds. One pocket for my ID card, the other for cash and mobile, a shoulder bag for water, notepad, pens, scarf and tissues. A tight T-shirt with a loose shirt on top and then a looser cardigan. The layered look – so if you're grabbed you can shed clothing and not be naked. A scrunchie and shades, cotton socks and flat shoes and you're ready for anything.

The phone keeps ringing. London, Montreal, Delhi, Dublin, the world wants to know how it feels to be in Tahrir and I keep saying I don't know because I'm not there. But over a million people are.

I'm writing and pacing. Writing and hedging. Will it be a piece about how we're free? Or a piece about how we're waiting, holding on? Pacing and answering the phone. Keeping an eye on the TV. Tahrir is the centre of the universe and it's ten minutes away and I'm not there. I go out on to the balcony. The street is deserted. The bats flit in and out of the mango trees. I write another paragraph. Pace and check my bag and pockets.

6.00 p.m.

It happens. A brief statement delivered by Omar Suleiman looking even deader than usual, with a scowling, heavy-set man in the frame behind him: Hosni Mubarak has stepped aside; the armed forces are in control of the country. My heart is pounding and my hands are freezing. I'm so – so full I think I shall burst. I rush back to the table and look at what I've written. I can hardly read but I know it won't do. I sit down, screw my eyes shut and take several deep breaths. Then I start again:

'In Tahrir Square and on the streets of Egypt the people

have reclaimed their humanity. Now they will reclaim their state . . . As of this minute there is no embezzling president, no extraordinary-rendition-facilitator Vice-President, no corrupt Cabinet, no rigged Parliament, no brutal emergency laws, no – regime! We have entered a new phase. For two weeks the people have been chanting: "The People! / The Army! / One Hand!". We will now work to make this true in the most positive way possible: that the army will guarantee peace and safety while we put in place the civilian structures that will help us to articulate how we want to run our country . . . In Tahrir I had met two women in the last stages of pregnancy. They were due to give birth any day and they wanted to give birth in a free Egypt. Now they can have their babies . . . The world has been watching this struggle between a tenacious, brutal and corrupt government, using all the apparatus of the state, and a great and varied body of citizens, armed with nothing but words and music and legitimacy and hope. The support of the world came through to us loud and clear, and what has happened here over the last two weeks will give voice and power to civilian citizens everywhere . . . Our work will begin now: to rebuild our country in as exemplary a fashion as the one in which we've won it back. To remember our young people who died that this night might happen and to carry them forward with us into a future good for us and good for our friends and good for the world . . . Look at the streets of Egypt tonight; this is what hope looks like.' Press SEND.

I emerge from Mesa7a Street straight into a traffic jam in Midan el-Gala2; everybody's trying to get to Tahrir. I sit with my windows open to the drumming, the happiness. It's a party; joy cries ring out constantly, people are dancing and jumping up and down on the traffic roundabout, dancing on the roofs of their cars, handing out candy. A man walks around with a tray handing out wedding sherbet. Kids are climbing lamp posts to wave their flags from the highest point possible. I call my sister, my father, Omar, Ismail, Lulie. I call Osta Ashraf: we've done it! We've done it! We've done it! We've done it! We only inch forward from time to time but we don't mind.

You can hardly see the lions on Qasr el-Nil for the kids climbing on to them. All the mobiles held high; everybody being photographed in the moment. I'm part of the surge of happy humanity flowing across the bridge. Beneath us, our river, alight with sparkling lights, with fireworks, with song. Then, Tahrir.

You breathe deep when you get to Tahrir. A steady roar rises from it and there are more fireworks and a million flags are waving and banners fly: 'No More Torture!' 'Welcome to Tomorrow!' 'Congratulations to the World!' And as I walk into the Midan the song that welcomes me from every loudspeaker is Abd el-Haleem's 1962 'bel-Ahdan': In our a-arms, in our a-arms, in our a-arms, in our arms our lovely country in our a-arms . . .' The last time I'd heard this song had been in 2005 in the great auditorium of the Opera House and the whole auditorium had wept in desolation, now I see us all here: we're crying and laughing and jumping and hugging and singing and then 'Watani Habibi' comes on, the pan-Arab anthem that's been forbidden for decades and everyone knows it by heart and roars along: 'In Palestine and the

rebellious south / We'll bring back your freedom for you',
and gentler, 'We're a nation that protects not threatens /
We're a nation that maintains not destroys' and now the
Ultras are circling the Midan, their energy like an electric
current fizzing off the walls of the Arab League. 'Everyone who loves Egypt / Come and help fix Egypt', off
the Mugamma3 building, 'We'll get married / We'll have
kids', off the Egyptian Museum, 'Lift your head up high,
you're Egyp-tian. Lift your head up high, you're Egyptian. Lift your head up . . .'

And in the centre of the Midan a stillness. The pictures
of the murdered. The shuhada. Sally Zahran, massive blows
to the head, glances upwards and smiles. Muhammad Abd
el-Menem, shot in the head, his hair carefully gelled. Ali
Muhsin, shot, carries a laughing toddler with a big blue sea
behind him. Muhammad Bassiouny, shot, lies back with
his two kids. Muhammad Emad holds his arms open wide
and wears a 'LONDON' T-shirt. Islam poses against the
Nile. Ihab Muhammadi smiles but his eyes are thought-
ful . . . and more, 843 more. In the triumph and joy and
uncertainty of the moment, they are the still centre; the
young people, the shabab, who walked into the Midan, in
peace, to save their country and to save us. Our future has
been paid for with their lives. There is no turning back.

Epilogue

On 12 February, the sun shone on Tahrir and the shabab came down and cleaned up after their revolution. Volunteers who arrived at the Midan after midday found it spick and span, and started cleaning up other streets instead. I saw kids perched on the great lions of Qasr el-Nil Bridge buffing them up.

I wrote then: 'I feel – and every parent will know what I mean – I feel that I need to keep my concentration trained on this baby, this newborn revolution – I need to hold it safe in my mind and my heart every second – until it grows and steadies a bit. Eighty million of us feel this way right now. Eighty million at least – because the support we've been getting from the world has been phenomenal. There's been something different, something very special, about the quality of the attention the Egyptian revolution has attracted: it's been – personal. We have a lot to learn very quickly. But we're working. And the people, everywhere, are with us.'[35]

Tunis are having their elections now. The Libyans have got rid of their regime. Yemen and Syria are still fighting. People are on the move in almost every country in the world. On 25 October, the people of Oakland, California, chanted: 'The People Demand the Fall of this Regime'; they chanted it in Arabic: 'al-Sha3b Yureed Isqat al-Nizam.' And on the 27th, Egyptians marched to the American Embassy in support of Occupy Oakland.

Events in Egypt, as we all know, did not go in a beautiful straight line from our Tahrir days to a truly representative government implementing the empowerment of the people. So we're still fighting. And this book is part of my fight, my attempt to hold our revolution 'safe in my mind and my heart'.

Today, 31 October, I'm specifically trying to hold Alaa Abd el Fattah, my nephew, safe in my mind and in my heart. It's two thirty in the afternoon and I'm walking with my sister, Laila, his mother, across the bridge from the Manial Palace to the Corniche. She's just finished classes and I've just put some visiting friends into a car for the airport and we're headed for the Appeals Prison in Bab el-Khalq. Alaa is in there. He came back from San Francisco on Saturday and presented himself at the Military Prosecutor's on Sunday morning, yesterday. His father, Ahmad Seif, and other lawyers were with him. He presented himself and said to the Prosecutor that he would not submit to the investigation for two reasons: because he believes that civilians should not be tried before military courts, and because the military is itself one of the accused in the Maspero case and therefore cannot also be both prosecutor and judge. The Prosecutor decided to jail him pending trial. The lawyers argued that he had come to the court of his own free will, returning from abroad to do so, that he has a known address and family, and that his wife is due to have their baby in three weeks – so he isn't going to run away. But they locked him up for the maximum they could: fifteen days renewable.

We walk between the 'French' Qasr el-Eini Hospital where they saved my father's life five years ago and the Cancer Institute where Lulie did years of training, avoid Zeinhom Bridge which would take us to our madfan, cut across Sayyeda Zeinab Metro Station with my sister laughing at the municipality's 'pathetic attempts to modernise Cairo by means of shopping malls' and start cutting through the back streets towards Bab el-Khalq. It's cool and shady. The narrow streets are alive with business and chatter and laid back with coffee shops and men playing dominoes or backgammon. Laila comments on how the older districts of Cairo are oriented so you catch the slightest breeze as you walk through the streets. The city takes us over with its permanent hum, its impossible pavements, its dusty trees, the fruit barrows with oranges, guavas, pears, mangoes, pomegranates – all polished and arranged with such neat precision, its laundry hanging on clothes lines all organised with even the socks in pairs, its people – sending out that current that includes us in every group that we pass. I say to Laila: 'We're on our way to meet Manal outside the jail where they've locked up Alaa. We're carrying blankets and books and a light and soap because he has none of these things. We don't even know if they'll give them to him. And yet, I don't feel horrid any more; these streets are making me feel everything will be OK.' 'Yes,' she says, 'and look at this.' And 'this' is a massive thirteenth-century mosque that rises up to our right, so at home, so relaxed, that I hadn't

even noticed it. Red plastic chairs stacked in one of its
doorways lead the eye up to the exquisite dovetailed
stonework that arches over it, a bright makeshift awning
attached to one of its walls is shelter for a tea stall. Laila
and I stop for a moment, adjust and shift each other's
burdens, and walk on.

My father says we shall prevail, because 'we' are a
people fighting for what's right, and 'they' are a faction
fighting for a sliver of gain. Well, you, as you read, know
a great deal more than I can know now. There are many
bad possibilities. But there are more good ones. I believe
that optimism is a duty; if people had not been optimistic
on 25 January, and all the days that followed, they would
not have left their homes or put their wonderful, strong,
vulnerable human bodies on the streets. Our revolution
would not have happened.

And tonight, it's starting up again. We show up at
the march for Alaa in Tal3at Harb and by the time we
reach Tahrir it's three thousand people. We march down
Tahrir Street, through Abdeen to the prison where Laila,
Manal and I were earlier today. This is the neighbourhood surrounding one of the gateways of the old city:
Bab el-Khalq, the Gate of the Multitudes. We are three
thousand people outside the jail. Central Security have an
armed battalion facing us, and others down the side streets.
As our chanting and drumming grow louder the roof of
the prison is filled with plainclothes policemen peering
down at us. We stand for two hours chanting for Alaa and
all the shabab held unjustly, then we wind back into town.
We chant and distribute stickers and talk to people. Once
again we are reclaiming our streets.

And so I'll imagine that you're reading this page here, in Cairo; the capital of an Egypt that's come back to her people, that's regained control of her land, her resources and her destiny, an Egypt that is part of a world on its way to finding a better, more equitable and sustainable way of life for its citizens, where people's dreams and ambitions and inventiveness and imagination find an open horizon, and where variety and difference are recognised as assets in confident, vibrant, outward-looking communities.

We are fortunate – the world is fortunate – that we had the Tahrir days, that for eighteen days we lived the dream, and so we know – absolutely – that life can be that dream. And because it was the shabab who made this possible, because it was they who changed the world, and it now belongs to them, I want to leave you with some of their voices; the young Egyptians, the young Cairenes, who are working and living our revolution as I put down my pen.

Mona, 16 September 2011

There are fights one doesn't pick; you just find yourself in the middle of it and you have to perform.

My fight against Military Trials for Civilians began on 26 February, the day I was in a sit-in and saw the army beating up people spitefully and unjustly. I saw them grab a boy and take him behind their checkpoint and I knew he would be badly beaten like other shabab I saw, and if it wasn't for my mum and her strength that she insisted she would not leave until they let the boy go – and they let him go – if it wasn't for that I'd never have got up the courage to do what I'm doing and start on this story that's not finished yet.

My story is the story of that boy, Amr el-Beheiri, who they grabbed again after fifteen minutes.

They tried him quickly and in secret without notifying his family or his lawyer, and they sentenced him to five years in a very distant jail.

I got involved at the moment I was holding on to his arm and saying: 'Let's not leave him to go home alone. Let's take him with us.' And then I allowed them to convince me to let him get into the car and go with the others.

When I learned he'd been sentenced all I could think of was that I should not have let go of him. My mind keeps replaying the same shot: my hand letting go of his arm, letting him get into the car. I shouldn't have let him go; I should have listened to that voice inside me, that uneasy voice that said hold on to him.

But this is my story and this is my destiny and this is where I started.

The story got much bigger than Amr el-Beheiri: I came to discover twelve thousand Amrs, maybe more. But it all started with a personal incident that made me responsible for Amr el-Beheiri, and then the hundreds I stumbled on after that. From every new story that I hear there is a name that stays in my mind, that makes their pain my pain, their resistance my resistance, my voice their voice.

I am asking you to share their journey. And to take it personally.[36]

Alaa, 24 June 2011

Perhaps those who are not normally described as 'intel-
lectuals' don't know the terms 'narrative' and 'symbol' and
'discourse' – but the thing itself still affects them. 'The
people' are far more aware than many think. The people
know that Tahrir was simply spectacle. They know that
the revolution was won in the streets and the factories. But
they also know that the spectacle is important in the battle
of ideas, and if Tahrir falls, the dream falls. Tahrir is a myth
that creates a reality in which we've long believed.

We know nothing of the coming world but we are
certain of the destiny of the shuhada. Do we imagine that
God's mercy knows class? . . . The shuhada's parents are
not in search of justice for justice will not bring back the
shaheed; their search is for a dream that gives meaning to
their sacrifice; for a happy ending to a story that includes
their suffering.

The shuhada chose to fight the regime even though
they knew that summarising their problem in 'the regime'
was a myth. But it's a myth fed with belief and sacrifice;
a gamble that reality can be changed. They're not stupid.
Just as the shabab in front of the Israeli Embassy knew that
democracy alone will not face up to imperial injustice, the
poor naturally know that democracy alone never removed
poverty and the law courts alone never established justice
for the poor, and we have proof in the protests of the
workers of Wisconsin and the students of England.

Turn away from the experts and listen to the poets;
we're in a revolution. Beware of caution and embrace
the unknown; we're in a revolution. Put aside calcula-

tions and hold on to the dream; we're in a revolution. Celebrate the shuhada, for in the midst of the ideas, the symbols, the stories, the spectacles and the dreams nothing is real except their blood, and nothing is certain except their immortality.[37]

Sanaa and the editorial team of
al-Gurnal, 27 February 2011

On 25 January the Egyptian street started to move
for the first time in thirty years – under the leadership
of the shabab of Egypt. We are a group of shabab who
have lived through the changes that happened to us and
to others inside and outside Tahrir during the revolution.
We did different kinds of work: cleaning, traffic control,
guarding shops, securing streets . . . We transformed from
ordinary shabab focused on our daily lives into 'revolutionaries'. And when we saw how the media was employed to
confuse and mislead we decided to produce this newspaper
to counter the misuse of the media both inside Egypt and
outside it.

We want to move to a new stage. We don't want to be
sitting at computers, we want to be out on the streets with
the people. Why should freedom just be virtual? People
said we had to get a licence from State Security, and we
said no; we've had a revolution, now we don't ask for
permission, we establish freedom as facts on the ground.
We want to see different opinions literally on the same
page: an Ikhwan (Muslim Brotherhood), a Progressive and
a Liberal – all on the same page. We want debate.

To prove our complete commitment to freedom of
expression we will not affiliate ourselves to any political current. We pledge not to impose any opinion and
to welcome all articles, poems or artwork whatever their
point of view. Our aim is to guarantee that complete freedom of expression which we have been denied for so long.

P.S. in the Midan I dreamed of the fall of Mubarak and of elections, any elections – where my voice would matter. Mubarak fell and we have elections coming and I've just worked out I can't vote because I'm not eighteen yet.

Omar Robert, 13 February 2011

We made a city square powerful enough to remove a
dictator. Now we must re-make a nation to lead others on
the road to global equality and justice.

Tahrir Square worked because it was inclusive – with
every type of Egyptian represented equally. It worked
because it was inventive – from the creation of electric and
sanitation infrastructure to the daily arrival of new chants
and banners. It worked because it was open-source and
participatory – so it was unkillable and incorruptible. It
worked because it was modern – online communication
baffled the government while allowing the revolutionaries
to organise efficiently and quickly. It worked because it was
peaceful – the first chant that went up when under attack
was always 'Selmeyya! Selmeyya!'. It worked because it
was just – not a single attacking baltagi was killed, they
were all arrested. It worked because it was communal –
everyone in there, to a greater or lesser extent, was putting
the good of the people before the individual. It worked
because it was unified and focused – Mubarak's departure
was an unbreakable bond. It worked because everyone
believed in it.

Inclusive, inventive, open-source, modern, peaceful,
just, communal, unified and focused. A set of ideals on
which to build a national politics.[38]

★   ★   ★

Our story continues . . .

Notes

1 'At 22:34 UTC (00:34 a.m. local time), Renesys observed the virtually simultaneous withdrawal of all routes to Egyptian networks in the Internet's global routing table. Approximately 3,500 individual BGP routes were withdrawn, leaving no valid paths by which the rest of the world could continue to exchange Internet traffic with Egypt's service providers. Virtually all of Egypt's Internet addresses . . . unreachable . . ."
   http://gizmodo.com/5746121/how-egypt-turned-off-the-internet
2 http://www.youtube.com/watch?v=hWplnI-sWzs&feature=feedu
3 Throughout the nineteenth century, one of the many theatres to host the drama of British-French rivalry, was archaeology – and the stealing of antiquities – in Egypt. Successive Egyptian governments of the period consistently favoured the French. Three of the most important streets in the part of Cairo established by Khedive Ismail in the late nineteenth century are named after Frenchmen who made radical contributions to Egyptology: Jean François Champollion (1790-1832) who published his translation of the 7agar Rasheed (the Rosetta Stone) hieroglyphs in 1822. Auguste Mariette (1821-1881): for whom, in 1858, Khedive Ismail created the post of Director-General of

Excavations and Antiquities and so started the institutionalisation of archaeology in Egypt. His sarcophagus rests in the garden of the Egyptian Museum. Gaston Maspero, (1846–1916) who succeeded Mariette Pasha as Director-General of Excavations and Antiquities from 1880 to 1886 and 1899 to 1914. He superintended the move of the Egyptian Museum collection from Gizah to its new (and current) home in 1902. Present in Shadi Abd el-Salam's 1969 film, *al-Moumya* (the Night of Counting the Years).

4 'Shabab' derives from the root sh/b to grow. I love the word; it carries the same emotional load as 'youth' with an extra dash of vigour, and it's both classical and colloquial in all Arabic dialects. It's unusual in that in its colloquial use it's plural without a gender marker. It also carries with it lots of words to do with the progress of age; 'shabba' (he grew up), 'Shaba' (he grew old. Literally: his hair grew white), 'shayb' (white hair), 'shayeb' (an old man with white hair – generally used only if he's done something not befitting his age). Unpackaged it carries the signification of 'people, men and women, who are at the youthful stage of life with all its energy, hope, optimism, vigour, impulsiveness and love of life, and who are acting communally, together'.

5 http://www.youtube.com/watch?v=3luSbFP6oa8

6 http://www.youtube.com/watch?v=k8jrDxLs3lE&feature=related

7 Muhammad Lazoghli himself, the man whose statue stands at the centre of the Midan, was a young soldier who came to Egypt with Muhammad Ali at the beginning of the nineteenth century to re-establish Ottoman rule after the withdrawal of Napoleon. They say he was the brains behind the Citadel Massacre which got rid of the remnant leaders of the old Mameluke era. His life's work was to set up a modern Egyptian state in the face of a for-the-moment defeated French imperialism. Minister of Defence, Minister

of Finance and first Prime Minister of Egypt from 1808 to 1823, his statue – statesmanlike, bearded, robed – was sculpted many years after his death and posed for by an Egyptian water-carrier who resembled him.

8 'Over the past three decades, such arrests, detentions and kidnappings have become fairly common. People disappear. Friends hunt for them. Usually they are in the State Security Intelligence Bureau in Lazoghli Square in Cairo. They are generally held long enough to extract a confession. Their treatment ranges from insults, threats and beatings to fairly evolved methods of torture. Sometimes the person is not required to confess to anything; they are given a warning and let go. Sometimes the person dies. Mostly, they are sent to jail to await trial.

Human rights cannot be regional. The rule of law cannot be selective. Guantánamo, Belmarsh, Lazoghli and Facility 1391 in Israel are part of the same configuration; they stand together or – one hopes – fall together.'

Soueif, *The Guardian*, 9 March 2006

9 http://www.youtube.com/watch?v=ozadTZ4oJiE

10 http://en.wikipedia.org/wiki/Hisham_Mubarak_Law_ Center

11 http://www.youtube.com/watch?v=btXZMh5tHDA

12 Khaled Said was a young man killed by police in a cybercafé in Alexandria on June 6, 2010. Because he was an "ordinary" young man, i.e. middle class, and not a criminal nor an activist, and because his brother managed to get a photo of his face disfigured by his beating, he became a rallying point for the opposition to police brutality in Egypt.

13 http://www.youtube.com/watch?v=U94PCrdHG4w

14 Millioneyyah: adding the suffix 'eyya' to a noun makes an adjective. So, 'selm' is 'peace' and 'selmeyya' is 'peaceful'; millioneyya in this case is a million-person event.

15 The story went that on 31 January, the day the F-16s buzzed Tahrir, Mubarak had ordered the army to attack the protestors,

the hundreds of thousands of Egyptians in the streets and midans of the country. The story continued that the army had already conducted a poll among the middle-ranking officers, the men in the field who would have had to fire on the protestors, and learned that if the order came to shoot the officers would refuse. So, when given the order, Field-Marshall Tantawi had said: 'I can't do it, Mr President.' Field-Marshall Tantawi later (in October) testified that he had never received such an instruction from Mubarak. This left open the question why army spokespeople repeatedly boasted that army had not attacked the revolutionaries.

16 http://www.youtube.com/watch?v=6ft3YhEShfs (Major Ahmad Shuman)

17 Shaheed, plural: shuhada. Martyr. The root sh/h/d is 'to see' and 'to bear witness'. A 'witness', for example in a court case, is a 'shahed'. Being a 'shahed' is only part – a temporary part – of a person's identity or function. A 'shaheed' is someone who bears ultimate witness; someone whose sole function now is to bear witness.

18 Qur'an, Chapter 3, verse 169.

19 One of the major protest groups, named after a massive strike by Mahallah textile workers in 2008 where several people were killed by the police.

20 The First Great Quarrel amongst the 'patriotic political forces' after the revolution had been run under the heading 'The Constitution First'. When SCAF announced the transitional programme for the country it was:

1. Election of the two Houses of Parliament
2. Parliament chooses a 'Founding Committee' which writes the Constitution
3. Election of the President

All the political forces rushed off to create parties; some to activate existing parties that were in various conditions of decay or discreditation or division. One group saw the need to create a coalition. This was meant to be a coalition of civilian forces to negotiate with or confront or in any case be the civilian voice of the revolution addressing SCAF and the world. They called the First Conference of Egypt on 7 May. It was attended by some 5,000 people and was as close to broadly representative of Egypt as you could get – except that the Islamist currents were only represented by some of their shabab who were already moving away from their mainstream. On the economic front the Conference aligned itself with sustainable development and social justice and a more equitable distribution of wealth. It presented a strong paper on the Constitution – almost a draft document. And it declared the formation of the National Council.

The first meeting of the National Council was convened on 7 June, and by then it was already defined by one main feature: it was calling for change of the SCAF schedule already agreed by the people in a Referendum. Their position, put forward by some powerful lawmen and women, was how can we have elections without a Constitution? The Constitution is the foundation of everything. How can you start to build without a foundation?

But putting the 'Constitution First' would mean:

1. throwing out the results of the Referendum; the first democratic exercise the country had engaged in and whose results (agreeing to SCAF's schedule) represented 'The Will of the People'.
2. Postponing elections – thereby giving the secular parties more time to organise and to try to catch up operationally with the Ikhwan (the Muslim Brotherhood) who have much more presence on the ground.
3. Removing the possibility that the Constitution would ultimately be written by a Founding Committee chosen by a Parliament with an Islamist majority.

The 'Constitution First' would also mean keeping the country in limbo by maintaining the military in power for longer and postponing stability and an accountable government. The campaign for the 'Constitution First' split the country into:

1. Some powerful secular figures and new parties insisting on the Constitution First.
2. Islamist figures and parties insisting on respecting 'The Will of the People', as expressed in the response to the referendum, and abiding by the SCAF schedule.
3. Figures (mostly non-Islamist) who said that in an ideal world it would have made more sense to write the Constitution first but that in our current circumstances, with the military seizing more power every day, the Cabinet weak and paralysed and the revolution stalled, it would be best to move towards elections and an accountable government and write the Constitution later. This group was also unwilling to discredit the first democratic exercise the country had gone through – the Referendum.

Eventually, Group (A) came up with the idea of putting forward (a) proposals for the selection of the Founding Committee that would write the Constitution – to ensure that it was representative of the country as a whole and not just of whoever happened to have a parliamentary majority at the time – and (b) a document listing a set of 'Constitutional Principles' that everyone could agree would frame the Constitution.

Many individuals and organisations started putting forward proposals and ideas. This activity took away from the support for the Constitution First and so, eventually, Group (A) – without officially renouncing its position – started putting forward its own proposals.

By then, however, their distrust of and dislike for the Islamist trend had become so obvious, that the Islamists Group (B) announced that even these ideas were an attempt to subvert 'The Will of the People' and that it was firmly against them and would not bind itself to any pre-Constitutional documents or agreements whatsoever.

21 Shaheed: martyr. See note 17 above.

22 Mosireen: determined. A pun on 'misriyyeen': Egyptian. A group of independent film-makers who have set up a collective media centre. See http://mosireen.org/

23 http://www.cinerevolutionnow.com/2011/07/tahrir-cinema-needs-you.html

24 http://literaryrevolutions.wordpress.com/2011/07/19/tweetnadwa-real-hope-for-egypts-future/

25 http://www.youtube.com/watch?v=ilyJAAwG74U (Testimony)

26 Ahmad al-Musallami, 'Al-Tabaa al-Oula', Dream TV, 17 September 2011.

27 http://en.nomiltrials.com/2011/10/egypt-end-military-trials-for-civilians.html

28 http://www.youtube.com/watch?v=jx33QyWZo2s&feature=youtu.be (Bloody Wednesday)

29 Eye witness report: 'On the 3rd of February 2011 at about 2.30 p.m. an individual claiming to be the Azbakeyya investigation inspector broke into HMLC ordering everybody there to sit on the floor. He was followed by a military Police lieutenant accompanied by two Military Police officers where the former stood on a chair and shouted: I have orders to shoot anybody who moves. A huge group of thugs then entered the centre accompanied by an intelligence officer. They searched the place, destroyed files and stole some of them, destroyed desks and took papers and CDs, searched personal bags of staff all the while throwing obscenities and accusations of destroying Egypt and conspiring with foreigners.

'After six hours of insults, verbal abuse, accusations of treason and tying the hands of staff members with leather strings the detainees were taken to the central administration of the Military Police in Khalifeh el Maamun in Heliopolis where their names were taken and photos and videos taken of them. They were then transported to some headquarters in Madinet Nasr, assumed to be one of the headquarters of Military Intelligence where they were interrogated while blindfolded. They were released three days later.

'As for the centre, windows, doors, desks, drawers and file cabinets were destroyed. Two computers, a printer, fax machine, router and a scanner disappeared.'

30 http://www.3quarksdaily.com/3quarksdaily/2011/02/the-women-of-tahrir-square.html

31 http://www.youtube.com/watch?v=rgLlxOqi1Hg

32 http://www.youtube.com/watch?v=-ETbR8usFlUU

33 http://abcnews.go.com/ThisWeek/video/omar-suleiman-crisis-12852023

34 http://www.haaretz.com/news/diplomacy-defense/mubarak-slammed-u-s-in-phone-call-with-israeli-mk-before-resignation-1.342831

35 http://www.bbc.co.uk/news/world-middle-east-12393795

36 http://ma3t.blogspot.com/2011/09/blog-post_16.html.

37 http://www.manalaa.net.

38 http://www.cinerevolutionnow.com.

All links given are live at time of going to press, but if a video has been removed just search YouTube with keywords; somebody will have posted a similar one.

Ahdaf Soueif is the author of the bestselling *The Map of Love* (shortlisted for the Booker Prize in 1999 and translated into more than twenty languages), as well as the well-loved *In the Eye of the Sun* and the collection of short stories, *I Think of You*. Ms Soueif is also a political and cultural commentator, described by the *London Review of Books* as 'a political analyst and commentator of the best kind', whose clear-eyed reporting and analysis is syndicated throughout the world. A collection of her essays, *Mezzaterra: Fragments from the Common Ground*, was published in 2004, the year in which her translation (from Arabic into English) of Mourid Barghouti's *I Saw Ramallah* also appeared. She writes regularly for *the Guardian* in the UK and has a weekly column in *al-Shorouk* in Egypt. In 2007 Ms Soueif founded Engaged Events, a UK based charity. Its first project is the Palestine Festival of Literature (PalFest) which takes place in Jerusalem, Bethlehem, Ramallah, Nablus, Jenin and al-Khalil/Hebron.

www.palestinelitfest.org

A NOTE ON THE TYPE

The text of this book is set in Bembo. This type was first used in 1495 by the Venetian printer Aldus Manutius for Cardinal Bembo's *De Aetna*, and was cut for Manutius by Francesco Griffo. It was one of the types used by Claude Garamond (1480–1561) as a model for his Romain de l'Université, and so it was the forerunner of what became standard European type for the following two centuries. Its modern form follows the original types and was designed for Monotype in 1929.